SPECTRUM READING
Grade 2

W9-AHB-851

Table of Contents

A Dog for Marta

Read about Marta's surprise.

1 Marta was eating breakfast slowly. She was in no hurry because she didn't have school that day. The telephone rang. Marta's mom answered, "Yes, we can come today. We'll be over later this morning."

2 She turned to Marta and said, "That was Aunt Rosa. She has a wonderful surprise for you."

3 "She has a surprise for me? What is it?" asked Marta.

4 Mom said, "Aunt Rosa found a dog, and she trained it for you."

5 "A dog! Great!" shouted Marta, jumping up and knocking over her chair. She ran to the closet for her coat and shoes. As she headed for the car, Marta called, "I'm ready to get my dog!"

Knowing the Words

Write the story words that have these meanings.

1. good or great

_____
(Par. 2)

2. place to keep coats

_____
(Par. 5)

3. went that way

_____
(Par. 5)

Reading and Thinking

1. This story is mostly about

_____ Marta's chair.

_____ Marta's surprise.

_____ Marta's breakfast.

Words such as *he, she,* and *it* take the place of other words. Read these sentences. Then fill in the blanks.

Marta shouted as she ran.

She stands for *Marta* _____.

2. Her mom laughed as she talked.

She stands for _____.

3. My dad talked as he worked.

He stands for _____.

Marta Sees Nicky

What kind of dog does Marta get?

1 There stood Marta's dog! It was a little tan one with long hair and a short tail. The dog wiggled all over when it saw Marta.

2 "This dog likes me!" Marta said.

3 "Yes, she does," said Aunt Rosa. "I've been calling her Nicky."

4 "I like that name, Aunt Rosa. Come, Nicky," called Marta.

5 Right away, Marta felt a wet nose on her arm. She said, "Good girl, Nicky. I can see you are a well-trained dog."

6 "Here is the little book that helped me train her," Aunt Rosa said. "You may take it and her leash. Be sure to walk Nicky every day."

7 "I will, Aunt Rosa," Marta said. "I will take good care of her."

Reading and Thinking

Put each word in the right blank.

nose   hair   leash

1. She wiggled her _____.

2. My dog has a new _____.

3. Does Nicky have short _____?

Circle the right answer.

4. What will Marta do next?

    go to the library

    take Nicky home

    feed the birds

5. What helped Aunt Rosa train Nicky?

_____

Working with Words

Circle the best word for each sentence.
Then write it in the blank.

1. Nicky _____ to Marta.

    can   ran   pan

2. Marta walked her _____.

    dog   does   did

3. Nicky wiggled her _____.

    eat   each   ear

Nicky Takes a Walk

Read to see why Marta likes walking with Nicky.

1   Marta and Nicky were walking in the park. Marta's friends were walking their dogs, too. Nicky trotted next to Marta. Marta was proud of her dog. She wanted everyone to see Nicky. She called, "Lee, come and see my dog!"

2   Lee headed their way, but her dog, Bigfoot, wanted to play in the park. Bigfoot pulled on the leash and ran the other way. Lee chased him and shouted, "Come back!"

3   Marta called to her other friends. "Christy and Joe, this is my dog! Come see her!" Christy's and Joe's dogs were not trained. They ran around a tree.

4   As she started to pet Nicky's side, Marta said, "What a good dog you are! Maybe you can show those other dogs how to take a walk."

Knowing the Words

Write the story words that have these meanings.

1. someone you like a lot

_____
(Par. 1)

2. someone who can carry things

_____
(Par. 4)

Circle the three words in each line that belong together.

3. house   book   park   store

4. bark   fly   wiggle   jump

5. soup   lunch   dinner   breakfast

6. ball   friend   neighbor   aunt

Reading and Thinking

1. This story is mostly about

_____ Nicky and the mail.

_____ a bone for Nicky.

_____ Mom's surprise.

2. Why does Nicky bark so much?

_____

_____

_____

3. Can you think of a way to make Nicky stop barking?

_____

_____

A New Friend

What can be done to stop a barking dog?

1 The next day Marta met the mail carrier on the sidewalk. Then Marta and the carrier walked up to the house. Nicky watched, but she did not bark. Marta called, "Mom, have you met our mail carrier, Mrs. Smith?"

2 Mom walked outside and said, "I'm glad to know you, Mrs. Smith. May I get you a drink of water?"

3 Mrs. Smith said, "Yes, please."

4 "Do you like your work, Mrs. Smith?" Marta asked.

5 "Yes," she answered. "I like walking. I like talking to everyone, too."

6 Then Mrs. Smith looked at Nicky. She said softly, "Hello, girl."

7 Nicky's ears were back. She walked over and sniffed before she sat down quietly as if to say, "I'm glad you are my friend."

12

Some of these sentences are about **real** things, things that could happen. Write **R** by them. The other sentences are about things that could not happen, **make-believe** things. Write **M** by them.

1. ___ A dog can run and play.

2. ___ A house can talk.

3. ___ A dog likes bones.

4. ___ A dog likes to read.

5. Why does Mrs. Smith like her

job? _____

_____

Write each set of words in A-B-C order.

1. mail   bark   know

_____

_____

_____

2. work   ears   please

_____

_____

_____

3. friend   carrier   drink

_____

_____

_____

13

Nicky Helps Mom

Read to see how Nicky's barking helps Marta's mom.

1   Mrs. Smith was gone, but Marta and her mom were still talking. Mom looked around and said, "We need to cut this grass today, Marta."

2   Then Nicky started to bark. She barked at Marta's mom and then ran back to the house. Mom said, "Oh, no, my bread! It will be burned!"

3   She ran into the kitchen and threw open the oven. There were the pans of bread. The bread was brown, but it was not burned. The family could still eat it.

4   Mom said, "Nicky, thank you for telling me the bread was done. When Marta called me, I walked out to see Mrs. Smith. I needed to hurry back in, but I didn't."

5   "Mom is right, Nicky. Sometimes barking is the right thing for a dog to do," Marta laughed as she petted Nicky.

Reading and Thinking

Put each word in the right blank.

started   petted   burned

1. He _____ to go away.

2. The wood _____ well.

3. We _____ the cat.

Write **R** by the sentences that are about **real** things. Write **M** by the sentences about **make-believe** things.

4. ____ Dogs can bake bread.

5. ____ People can bake bread.

6. ____ People bake bread in an oven.

7. ____ An oven keeps food cool.

Working with Words

A **base** word is a word without an ending. The words in each row have the same **base** word. Circle the ending of each one. Then write the **base** word in the blank.

1. calling   2. burning
   called   burned
   calls   burns

_____   _____

Circle the best word for each sentence. Then write it in the blank.

3. We'll eat _____ he comes.
   then   when   check

4. Please finish _____ apples.
   chase   those   shoes

Splash!

Where is it cool on a warm day?

1   Marta and Lee were tired from playing with their dogs. "Stop for a while!" shouted Lee. But Nicky and Bigfoot were not tired at all.

2   Then Marta said, "I've got an idea! It's cool at the creek. Why don't we go there to play?"

3   Lee said, "Great idea!" Soon they were heading for the creek. When they got there, Nicky sniffed the water where she saw little fish that could swim fast. All at once, Nicky jumped on one. Splash! When the water was quiet, Nicky looked for the fish. Where did it go?

4   Nicky didn't look for long. She soon found how much fun it was just to swim and splash. Marta laughed, "You look so funny when you are all wet, Nicky. Isn't it great to keep cool at the creek?"

Reading and Thinking

1. Marta and Lee went to the

creek because _____

_____.

2. Why couldn't Nicky find any

fish after she jumped in? _____

_____

3. Write **1, 2,** and **3** by these
sentences to show what
happened first, next, and last.

____ Nicky jumped into the
water.

____ Lee said, "Stop for a
while!"

____ Nicky sniffed the water.

Learning to Study

Write each set of words in A-B-C
order.

1. tired   idea   creek

_____

_____

_____

2. quiet   sniffed   fish

_____

_____

_____

3. splash   cool   jumped

_____

_____

_____

Neighbors

Do you think it's hard to make new friends? Does Marta?

1 "Get the ball, Nicky," said Marta. She threw it hard, and the ball flew high over the backyard fence. "Oh, no," said Marta. "Nicky, stay. I will get the ball."

2 Before Marta could move, a boy said, "Isn't this your ball?" He started to carry it to the fence.

3 "Yes, thanks," said Marta, as she took the ball. Marta threw it again for Nicky to chase.

4 The boy watched and said, "Does your dog know lots of tricks?"

5 Marta answered, "Yes, she does. I work with her a lot. You just moved here, didn't you?"

6 The boy nodded and said, "Yes, we moved here yesterday. My name is Mike. I have a collie, and his name is Flash. I would like him to know how to do tricks."

7 Marta said, "I'm Marta. This is Nicky. We want to be good neighbors. We can help you with Flash."

Knowing the Words

Write the story words that have these meanings.

1. run after

   _____
   (Par. 3)

2. moved the head up and down

   _____
   (Par. 6)

3. people who live near you

   _____
   (Par. 7)

Put a check by the meaning that fits the underlined word in each sentence.

4. Is it <u>hard</u> to make new friends?

   _____ something not soft

   _____ something not easy to do

5. I will <u>watch</u> Nicky play.

   _____ thing that tells time

   _____ look at

Reading and Thinking

1. What kind of dog is Flash?

   _____

2. This story is mostly about

   _____ Marta playing with Nicky.

   _____ a new neighbor.

   _____ Nicky's ball.

3. How will Nicky and Marta help

   Mike with his dog? _____

   _____

   _____

4. Flash can't do any tricks

   because _____

   _____.

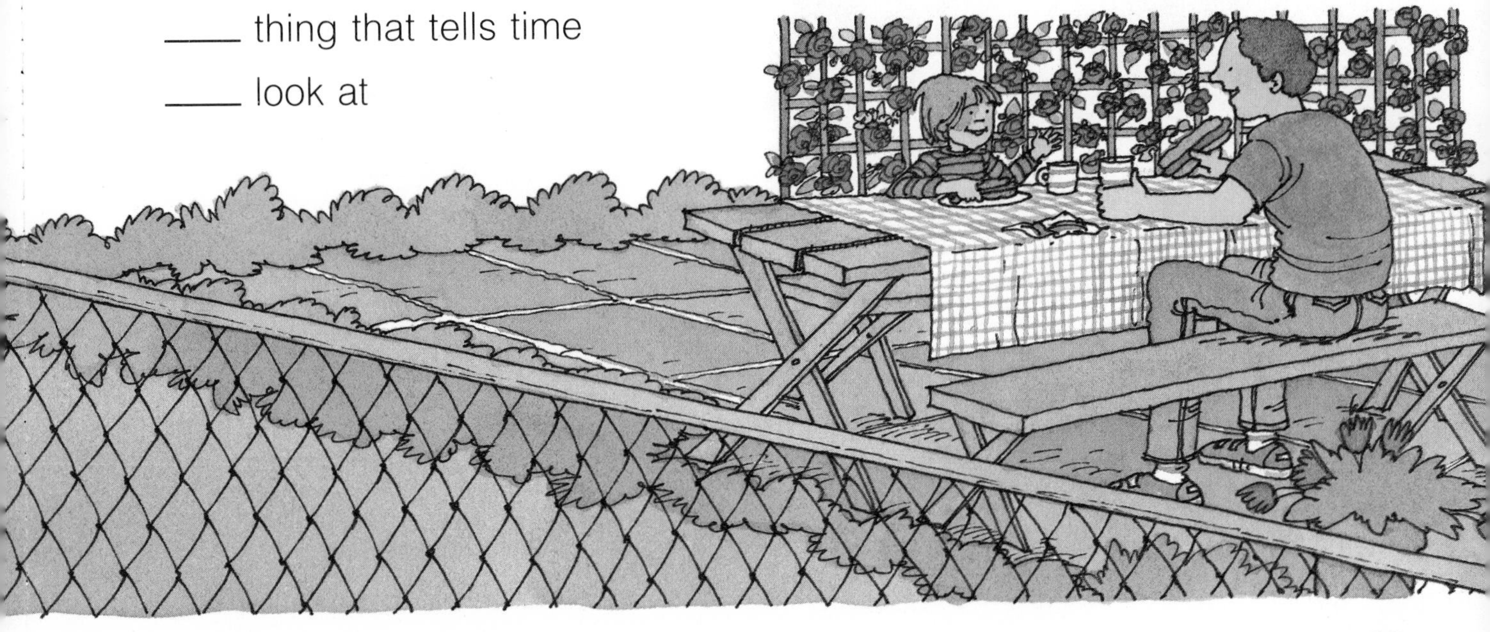

Nicky Runs Away

Read to see why Nicky runs away.

1   "Here we are, Nicky," said Marta. "I will take off your leash. You can run, but stay in the park."

2   As soon as Marta said this, Nicky started to run down the street. She ran into a big car lot. Marta chased her, shouting, "Come, Nicky!"

3   Nicky was barking at four dogs that were barking, too. On top of a car, a little black cat with big eyes sat and shook. The dogs couldn't get to it, but the cat couldn't get away.

4   Nicky growled at one big dog, which turned and ran. The other dogs saw Marta and ran, too.

5   Then Nicky sat next to the car and waited. Marta walked up and gave Nicky a big smile. "Good dog, Nicky. You chased away those mean dogs," she said as she helped the little cat down.

Reading and Thinking

1. This story is mostly about

    ____ Nicky playing.

    ____ Nicky finding a kitten.

    ____ Nicky holding a kitten.

2. The four dogs were barking

    because _____

    _____ .

3. What makes you think that

    Nicky likes kittens? _____

    _____

    _____

Working with Words

Circle the best word for each sentence. Then write it in the blank.

1. This _____ likes me.

    cat   call   cut

2. I will _____ a drink.

    gave   got   get

Write -**ing** or -**ed** in each blank.

3. I talk _____ with her yesterday.

4. She want _____ to work.

5. Now she is help _____ us.

Circle the right word for each sentence. Then write it in the blank.

6. Mike is my best _____.

    ground   proud   friend

7. I need a _____ of water.

    trick   drink   break

Nicky Comes Home

What does Nicky bring home?

1   Marta's dad had dinner almost ready. Did he hear a noise outside? When he looked, he saw Nicky with a furry black thing in her mouth. "Nicky, what do you have there?" asked Dad.

2   Nicky walked in and set the thing on the floor. It wiggled and made a little noise. When it stood up, Marta's dad saw that it was a wet kitten. He picked it up as Marta's mom walked into the room.

3   "It isn't hurt, just very wet," Dad told her.

4   Mom said, "It's so little that I think it still needs a mother. Nicky, will this be your own pet cat?" Nicky's tail pounded the floor.

5   Then Marta ran into the room. She had been listening as her mom and dad talked. Marta said, "I knew you would let it stay!"

Reading and Thinking

Look at each picture and circle the sentence that goes with it.

1. Nicky is playing outside.

   Nicky is playing in the house.

2. Nicky sleeps on Marta's bed.

   Nicky sleeps in her basket.

3. Who fixed dinner? _____

4. How did Nicky carry the kitten?

   _____

5. Why did Marta stay outside?

   _____

Working with Words

Circle the best word for each sentence. Then write it in the blank.

1. Nicky's collar has a _____.

   tag   than   tail

2. Nicky can be a _____ dog.

   get   quiet   paint

3. The little kitten was _____.

   pet   met   wet

Write these sentences. Use one of the shorter words from the box to stand for the words that are underlined.

| we'll   isn't   can't   didn't   I'm |

4. We will be there.

   _____

5. He did not go.

   _____

6. The kitten is not hurt.

   _____

7. I am hungry.

   _____

8. Flash cannot do tricks.

   _____

The Kitten Stays

Read to see whom the kitten likes best.

1   Marta's dad was still holding the little kitten. "We need to talk, Marta. Does this kitten belong to anyone?"

2   Marta answered, "I don't think so. Nicky and I found it at the car lot. Please, may we keep it?"

3   "Tomorrow," said Dad, "you should go back there and tell them our telephone number. If no one calls for the kitten, you may keep it."

4   "Good idea," said Marta's mom. "For now, warm some milk for this hungry kitten. I will make a bed."

5   Marta's mother found a little box and lined it with a soft blanket. "The kitten should like this bed," she said. "It's just right for him."

6   But the kitten had ideas of his own. When Marta's mom looked into the room that night, he was in Nicky's basket. The kitten was sleeping between Nicky's paws.

Reading and Thinking

1. This story is mostly about

   _____ warming the milk.

   _____ talking about dogs.

   _____ the kitten's new home.

Fill in the blanks.

2. Mom said, "Good idea,"
   as she warmed the milk.

   She stands for _____.

3. Mom found a box and lined it
   with a blanket.

   It stands for _____.

Working with Words

Circle the best word for each sentence. Then write it in the blank.

1. The milk is too _____.

   hit   hot   hat

2. The kitten's eyes are _____.

   big   bag   buy

3. Marta's mom made a _____.

   back   bed   bird

4. They have a _____ pet.

   now   not   new

Read these words and look at the pictures.

Marta's mom   her mom's hand

You can see that you add 's when you want to show that the hand belongs to Mom. Now write these names the same way.

5. Marta _____ hand

6. Mike _____ hand

25

The Pet Doctor

Why does Marta take her pet to the doctor?

1   Nicky, Marta, and the kitten were playing ball. Marta's dad walked into the room. "Marta, it looks as if you have fun with your pets," he said.

2   "I do, Dad. Nicky and I really like this kitten. We call him Inky."

3   "That is a good name for a black cat," her dad laughed. "Marta, we need to take Nicky and Inky to the doctor. We want them to stay healthy." Soon Marta, Dad, Nicky, and Inky were heading for the pet doctor.

4   A woman showed them to a little room, and the doctor came in to check Nicky and Inky. Her hands felt their soft coats. She looked into their eyes, ears, and mouths. Then she said, "I can tell that you take good care of your pets. Keep up the good work!"

5   Marta said, "I will do my best to keep them healthy."

Write the story words that have these meanings.

1. someone who keeps you well

_____
(Par. 3)

2. to be well

_____
(Par. 3)

3. to look over with care

_____
(Par. 4)

Circle the three words in each line that belong together.

4. arms   flowers   feet   hands

5. eyes   ears   doctor   mouth

6. hair   brown   white   black

1. This story is mostly about

____ pets who are not well.

____ a mean doctor.

____ keeping pets healthy.

2. What four things did the doctor check on Nicky and Inky?

_____

_____

_____

_____

3. What do you think Marta can do to keep her pets healthy?

_____

_____

27

A Rainy Day

What can happen on a rainy day?

1 "Why did it have to rain?" said Marta. "Today we were going to start the dog-training lessons. Now there is nothing to do."

2 Then there was a knock on the door. Nicky barked and ran over to it. The knock sounded again, and Nicky pounded her tail on the floor. Slowly Marta walked to the door.

3 There stood her friends Lee, Joe, Christy, and Mike with a boy Marta didn't know. Mike said, "Marta, this is my friend Allen. He just got a new puppy."

4 Joe said, "We need lessons in dog training just as much as our dogs do. It was raining too much to work outside. We thought we could learn a lot working here with Nicky."

5 Nicky barked and wiggled all around. Marta said, "Come in, everyone. We won't let a little rain stop us, will we?"

Reading and Thinking

Put each word in the right blank.

puppy   learn   door

1. Please open the _____.

2. Children _____ at school.

3. My _____ has black eyes.

4. Write **1, 2,** and **3** by these sentences to show what happened first, next, and last.

   _____ Marta was glad to see her friends.

   _____ Nicky barked and ran to the door.

   _____ There was a knock on the door.

Working with Words

Circle the best word for each sentence. Then write it in the blank.

1. Can you read this _____?

   cook   look   book

2. Marta _____ Allen today.

   mail   met   mean

3. Nicky pounded her _____ on the floor.

   tail   fill   well

The missing word in each sentence sounds like *right*. Change the *r* in *right* to *f, l,* or *n*. Write the new words. The first one is done.

4. *fight* _____ _____

Use the words you made in sentences.

5. Please turn off the _____.

6. We will not _____ over the toys.

7. It rained last _____.

A Lesson for Lee

Is it easy to train a dog?

1 Marta started with an easy lesson. She said, "First, your dog needs to know its name. When it comes, pet it a lot like this." Then Marta called, "Nicky, come!" When Nicky did, Marta petted her and said, "Good dog!"

2 Everyone but Lee thought it was a good trick. She said, "That is easy!"

3 Marta said, "Now you try it."

4 Lee called loudly, "Here, Nicky," but Nicky did not move at all.

5 Marta said, "She knows only one word for every trick. Say *come.*"

6 Lee said, "Well, I will try it. Nicky, come." Nicky trotted right over to Lee, and Lee said in surprise, "She did it!"

7 Marta didn't smile but said, "You have to show her you are glad she did it. That is important."

8 Lee petted Nicky on the head and said, "Oh, Nicky, you good dog!"

9 Marta laughed and asked, "Lee, will it be as easy to train your dog as it was to train you?"

Reading and Thinking

Put each word in the right blank.

     special   bath   letter

1. Why is today so _____?

2. Nicky likes her _____.

3. Marta wrote a _____.

4. Who trained Nicky to sit?

_____

5. What is going to happen soon?

_____

6. This letter is mostly about
   ____ Marta and her friends.
   ____ the special trick.
   ____ Nicky.

Learning to Study

Write each set of words in A-B-C order.

1. trained   bath   special

_____

_____

_____

2. care   splash   trick

_____

_____

_____

3. pet   basket   sleeps

_____

_____

_____

Mail for Marta

Who sent a letter to Marta?

Dear Marta,

¹ Thank you for your letter. It came in today's mail, and we were delighted to hear from you.

² We would love to come to your dog show. It will be a lot of work for you to put on a show. Are your friends going to help? Will you surprise everyone with that special trick then?

³ It's good that you know how to give Nicky a bath. That way you can always keep her clean.

⁴ When your mother was a girl, she had a dog, too. That dog used to hide your mother's things. Does Nicky hide your things?

⁵ We can't wait to see Nicky's pet kitten. Does Inky still like Nicky best? Nicky and Inky seem to be special friends.

⁶ We'll be seeing you soon.

Love,
Grandmother
and Grandfather

Reading and Thinking

Put each word in the right blank.

hide   clean   delighted

1. My hands are _____.

2. I am _____ to see you.

3. Will Nicky _____ this bone from me?

4. Why do you think that Marta's grandmother and grandfather like dogs? _____

_____

Working with Words

Circle the best word for each sentence. Then write it in the blank.

1. Nicky has a cold _____.

    nose   not   now

2. We will _____ a walk.

    talk   take   tail

The missing word in each sentence sounds like *make*. Change the *m* in *make* to *b, t,* or *w*. Write the new words.

3. _____   _____   _____

Use the words you made in sentences.

4. May we _____ a walk?

5. I like to _____ bread.

6. Did Nicky _____ you?

You know that *Mom's hand* means "the hand of Mom." Add *'s* when you write these names to show what belongs to each.

7. Dad   _____ coat

8. Mike   _____ book

9. Nicky   _____ teeth

Nicky Plays with Dad

Read to see what game Nicky and Dad are playing.

1 Every morning Marta, her mom, and her dad worked around the house. Each one always did the same job.

2 Marta cleaned up the breakfast dishes. Inky stayed with Marta to help clean up any milk. Marta's mom worked in the garden while the day was still cool. Her dad made the beds, and Nicky would try to help.

3 To make a bed, Marta's dad pulled the blankets from one side and then the other. One day when he shook the top blanket, the end of it brushed Nicky's nose.

4 Nicky liked that—a new game! Dad was playing with her! Nicky jumped up and pulled on the blanket with her mouth. Dad shouted, "Let go, Nicky! Give me that blanket."

5 Playing with Marta's dad was so much fun. Nicky shook the blanket and growled.

6 Dad picked up a newspaper and hit the floor with it. This time Nicky let the blanket go. She did not like that noise. She understood that Marta's dad was not playing.

Knowing the Words

Write the story words that have these meanings.

1. work you do

_____
(Par. 1)

2. made a low sound

_____
(Par. 5)

Put a check by the meaning that fits the underlined word in each sentence.

3. The blanket will <u>brush</u> Nicky's nose.

_____ thing used to fix hair

_____ move over softly

4. Will Dad <u>play</u> with Nicky?

_____ have fun

_____ a show

Reading and Thinking

1. Who cleaned up after

breakfast? _____

2. How did Inky help? _____

_____

Write **R** by the sentences that are **real** things. Write **M** by the sentences that are about **make-believe** things.

3. _____ People can make beds.

4. _____ Dogs can make beds.

5. _____ Cats can weed flowers.

6. _____ People can weed flowers.

Nicky Gets Wet

What is Nicky's surprise?

1   At last Marta had the sidewalk clean, so she put the broom away. Marta's mom was done weeding the flowers, too.

2   "Now we must water the grass," said Mom. "The ground is dry, and the grass needs water."

3   Marta helped her mother put the watering hose in the yard. Then they walked up to the house to turn on the water.

4   "Come, Nicky!" Marta shouted. "You had better stand back."

5   But Nicky wanted to see what was on the grass. She sniffed the hose. What was this funny thing in the yard? How still it was!

6   The thing started to get big. When it was big enough, it sent water up in little streams. Water went all over the grass, and all over Nicky, too.

7   Nicky jumped back. She liked most surprises, but not this one. She opened her mouth to bark, and water flew into it. Wet, wet Nicky! There was water on her and water in her!

Reading and Thinking

Put each word in the right blank.

streams   hose   dry

1. We use a _____ to water our flowers.

2. _____ of water ran down the window.

3. Is the paint _____?

Write **R** by the sentences that are about **real** things. Write **M** by the sentences about **make-believe** things.

4. ____ A yard can walk.

5. ____ A dog can walk.

6. ____ Birds can fly.

7. ____ Dogs can fly.

Working with Words

Circle the best word for each sentence. Then write it in the blank.

1. She likes to _____ flowers.

    pet   pan   pick

2. Sit _____ and read.

    back   bake   best

3. I like _____ book.

    think   thank   that

Fill in the missing vowel (*i, o,* or *u*) so the sentence makes sense.

4. Write on the l___ne.

5. Please give Nicky a b___ne.

6. May Nicky ___se this pan?

Fill in each blank with **str** or **spr** so the sentence makes sense.

7. Here is a ball of _____ing.

8. I will _____ay the grass.

9. Don't walk in the _____eet.

Helping Others

Why will Marta ride her bicycle today?

1   One day Mike's mother called Marta on the telephone. She said, "Marta, I need some things from the store. Mike can't go now. Could you get the things for me?"

2   "I will ask my mom," Marta said.

3   Her mother said yes, so Marta rode over to Mike's house on her bicycle. Nicky walked with her. Mike's mother gave Marta some money. "Marta," she said, "my things won't cost this much. You may spend what is left."

4   At the store, Marta found the things for Mike's mother. Then she picked out a good bone for Nicky. She was looking at things for herself when she saw a red ball. Nicky had one, but Flash didn't. She got the ball for Flash. On the way home, the ball fell out of Marta's bag. She looked back to see where it was. Then she saw Nicky carrying Flash's ball.

5   Marta was glad to be helping her neighbors. Nicky was helping, too.

Reading and Thinking

Put each word in the right blank.

cost   spend   bicycle

1. I have a new _____.

2. I will _____ my own money.

3. Does this ball _____ much?

Fill in the blanks.

4. Flash's ball fell so Nicky carried it.

   It stands for _____.

5. Marta and Nicky were happy because they were helping.

   They stands for _____

   and _____.

6. Nicky was carrying the ball as she ran.

   She stands for _____.

Working with Words

Circle the best word for each sentence. Then write it in the blank.

1. Did Marta _____ Nicky?
   day   tail   train

2. Can you _____ Nicky bark?
   heel   hear   head

3. Put on your warm _____.
   coat   cook   clean

Change each underlined word to two words. Write them on the line.

4. Flash <u>didn't</u> have a ball.

   _____

5. This <u>isn't</u> my bicycle.

   _____

Circle the right letters for each sentence. Then write them in the blank.

6. I st_____ted to sit up.
   er   ar   ir

7. This book is too sh_____t.
   or   er   at

8. Did the salesp_____son help?
   or   er   ar

Mike's New Airplane

Read to see what happened to Mike's airplane.

1   One day Marta and Mike went to the toy store. Mike wanted something special. The salesperson showed them many toys. When they left the store, Mike owned an airplane that would really fly. He was proud of his new toy. He wanted to take good care of it.

2   Later Mike and Marta walked to the park to try the airplane. They took Flash and Nicky with them. Mike threw the airplane first. It floated over some evergreens and landed at his feet.

3   "See how easy it is, Marta. It is fun to watch. Now you try."

4   Marta threw the airplane, but she did not fly it right. The airplane floated for just a short time. Then it fell and hit Nicky! Nicky jumped up and barked at it. Then she picked it up and shook it.

5   Mike's new airplane couldn't be fixed! It would not fly again. Marta said, "Mike, I will buy you another airplane, and we won't let Nicky near it."

44

Knowing the Words

Write the story words that have these meanings.

1. moved on the air

_____
(Par. 2)

2. trees with leaves that stay green

_____
(Par. 2)

3. came to the ground

_____
(Par. 2)

Put a check by the meaning that fits the underlined word in the sentence.

4. Did Marta know how to throw the airplane <u>right</u>?

____ not on the left

____ not the wrong way

Reading and Thinking

Put each word in the right blank.

owned   proud   evergreens

1. I am _____ of my dog.

2. We planted _____ in our yard.

3. Mike _____ a new toy.

4. Write **1, 2,** and **3** by these sentences to show what happened first, next, and last.

____ Nicky shook Mike's toy.

____ Mike got an airplane.

____ Marta said that she would buy another airplane.

5. Why does Marta want to buy Mike a new airplane?

_____

_____

A New Game?

What is Nicky's new game?

1   One day Marta's mother was pulling weeds in the flower bed, and Marta wanted to help. "That looks like fun. May I do that, too?"

2   "No," Mom said. "You may not know which ones are going to be flowers and which ones are weeds. Sometimes it's hard to tell. If you want to help, you can sweep the sidewalk for me. Will you do that?"

3   "Sure, Mom," said Marta. She got the broom and started to sweep. Nicky ran to Marta because sweeping looked like a new game.

4   "Get out of the way, Nicky," said Marta. "You are standing right where I want to sweep." But Nicky thought Marta wanted to play. She did not understand. Every time the broom moved near her, Nicky jumped at it. At last Marta shouted, "Nicky, I'm trying to help Mom. Now stop!" She shook the broom at Nicky.

5   This time Nicky understood. Marta was not playing a new game.

Knowing the Words

Write the story words that have these meanings.

1. thing that shows pictures

_____
(Par. 1)

2. ideas or ways of doing

something _____
(Par. 1)

3. room used for cooking

_____
(Par. 1)

Put a check by the meaning that fits the underlined word in each sentence.

4. Nicky <u>can</u> shut the door.

_____ a thing to hold food

_____ knows how to

5. I must <u>check</u> for the newspaper.

_____ make a line

_____ look with care

Reading and Thinking

1. Why do you think Marta's dad didn't open the door himself?

_____

_____

2. Do you think Nicky will shut the

door again? _____

Why or why not? _____

_____

_____

3. Write **1, 2,** and **3** by these sentences to show what happened first, next, and last.

_____ Marta's dad looked for the newspaper.

_____ Marta's dad watched television.

_____ Marta saw Nicky's new trick.

Pop, Pop, Pop!

What can you do on a slow day?

1   Marta and her friends stood at the door of Mom's room. When Marta knocked, her mother said, "Yes?"

2   "What can we do?" asked Marta. "Tell us something new to do."

3   Mom said, "It's always fun to pop popcorn. Would you like to do that?"

4   "Oh, yes," answered the children. Mom told them what to do and watched as they worked. Soon the popcorn started to pop. Pop, pop, pop! A wonderful smell filled the kitchen.

5   Inky had been sleeping on top of the television. Now she jumped and landed on Nicky, who was sleeping on the floor. The kitten started to play with Nicky's paws. Nicky barked and wiggled. Everyone laughed, and Marta said, "The popping noise didn't wake Nicky, but Inky did!"

6   At last the popcorn was quiet. When Marta opened the top of the pan to look in, a piece jumped up and hit Nicky.

7   "Shut the top!" said Joe.

8   "You do it! I need to pet my poor dog!" laughed Marta.

Reading and Thinking

1. Why did Nicky wake up?

_____

_____

Put each word in the right blank.

wonderful   wake   piece

2. Warm bread smells

_____.

3. Please give me a _____ of bread.

4. Will you _____ me?

Working with Words

The missing word in each sentence sounds like *stop.* Change the *st* in *stop* to *t, m,* or *p.* Write the new words and put them in the right sentences.

1. _____ _____ _____

2. Some popcorn didn't _____.

3. I hit the _____ of my head.

4. Clean the floor with a _____.

Circle the right letters for each sentence. Then write them in the blank.

5. They walked in the p_____k.

er   ir   ar

6. What happened f_____st?

ar   or   ir

Add *'s* to these words to show what belongs to each one.

7. dog   the _____ collar

8. cat   the _____ head

9. bird   the _____ nest

10. kitten   the _____ ball

53

A Close Call

Read to see what happened to Flash.

1   Marta and Nicky were playing in the yard. All at once Marta saw Flash, Mike's dog, playing in the muddy park. She didn't see Mike at all. "That's funny," thought Marta. "Mike never lets Flash out alone." Flash was walking in the street when Marta saw a fast car.

2   Still no Mike! As loudly as she could, Marta shouted, "Flash, come!"

3   Right away, Flash ran to Marta. Flash was so glad to see her!

4   Marta threw her arms around him and said, "That was a close call. You almost got hurt, Flash. I'm glad Mike has been training you to come when he calls your name."

5   Marta was delighted that the dog lessons had helped Flash. As she petted him, Flash jumped up. Now Marta was muddy, too!

6   "We must hurry home," Marta told Nicky. "I've got to call Mike. I need to tell him that I found Flash and that we really need a bath!"

Knowing the Words

Write the story words that have these meanings.

1. near

   _____
   (Par. 4)

2. so glad

   _____
   (Par. 5)

Circle the three words in each line that belong together.

3. paws   tail   soft   head
4. glad   delighted   pleased   sad
5. paint   grass   park   yard

Reading and Thinking

1. This story is mostly about

   ____ a fast car.

   ____ Mike's bicycle.

   ____ Marta helping Flash.

2. Why was Flash walking in the

   street by himself? _____

   _____.

3. How had the dog lessons

   helped Flash? _____

   _____

4. Write **1, 2,** and **3** to show what happened first, next, and last.

   ____ Flash ran to Marta.

   ____ Marta called to Flash.

   ____ Marta played in her yard.

Better Than a Bath

Read to see what is better than a bath.

1   Marta put the two dogs in the backyard. Then she headed inside to call Mike and to wash off the mud.

2   Her dad met her at the back door and said, "Oh, no, you don't! Our house is clean right now, so you need to use the hose to wash off. This mud needs to stay outside where it belongs!" Then he shut the door.

3   Marta knocked on the door. When her dad opened it again, Marta said, "If I can't come in, will you call Mike and then hold the telephone for me so I can talk?" Soon she was saying, "Hello, Mike? Flash is here in my backyard."

4   Mike said, "You found him! Good!"

5   Marta went on, "Yes, now go and put on your swimsuit because you and I can wash our dogs with the hose. Flash and I are too muddy to take a bath inside."

6   Mike said, "All right. I will be right there."

7   Marta said, "Thanks, Dad! This is a much better idea than a bath. We'll have a good time and get the dogs clean, too."

Reading and Thinking

1. What did Marta think was

   better than a bath? _____

   _____

2. Why did Marta's dad help her

   call Mike? _____

   _____

Put each word in the right blank.

   belongs   mud   swimsuit

3. Flash has _____ on him.

4. This book _____ to Allen.

5. My _____ is too big.

Working with Words

Fill in the missing vowel (a, i, or o) so each sentence makes sense.

1. You did a f____ne job.

2. Wash off with the h____se.

3. We will m____ke the bed.

Use the underlined words to make a new word to finish each sentence.

4. A suit that you wear when you

   swim is called a _____.

5. A yard that is in back of a

   house is called a _____.

Circle the best word for each sentence. Then write it in the blank.

6. Do not _____ at me.
   show   shout   chair

7. Our house is _____.
   boat   clean   stay

Inky Gets the Milk

Do you sometimes watch television on Saturday morning?

1 It was Saturday morning. Marta and her pets were watching television. Marta sat in a big chair eating her breakfast as she watched. Her big dish of Honey Corns was gone. Now she was eating an apple.

2 Inky found his ball and pushed it with his paw. Nicky barked and started to chase the ball. Marta picked it up, and said, "No, Nicky. Don't bark. Mom and Dad are still sleeping, so we have to be quiet. You sit here with me and watch television."

3 On television a cat with a hat was trying every way it could to get milk. It did lots of tricks. Not one of them worked. The funny cat was so hungry, but it couldn't get any milk.

4 Then Marta heard a lapping sound. She looked down to see Inky with his paws on the Honey Corns dish, drinking as fast as he could.

5 Marta said, "Inky, you should be on television. You could show that hungry cat a new trick so it could get some milk!"

Reading and Thinking

Put each word in the right blank.

quiet   lapping   television

1. The cat is _____ up the milk.

2. What _____ show do you like best?

3. We were _____ in the library.

4. This story is mostly about

    ____ Inky's trick.

    ____ Mom and Dad needing quiet.

    ____ Nicky wants to play.

Working with Words

To make a word mean more than one, add -es if the word ends in s, ss, ch, sh, or x. Write these words so that they mean more than one.

1. lunch   _____

2. dish   _____

3. box   _____

Fill in the missing letter so the sentence makes sense.

4. I like to h____lp my dad.

5. Nicky j____mped into the water.

6. Marta p____cked up the ball.

Fill in the missing letters so each sentence makes sense.

ar   or   ur

7. Did Nicky h_____t her paw?

8. Can we play in your y_____d?

Keep Away

How does Marta help her mom and dad?

1 Nicky and Marta were in the basement playing keep-away with an old football. Marta chased Nicky, but Nicky never let her take the ball. Each time Marta got near, Nicky ran faster. It was great fun!

2 Dad was not pleased with them. He and Mom were trying to paint an old table. "Marta, when you and Nicky run, you make the dust fly up. If your mother and I paint in dusty air, the paint will not look good. Please play outside until dinner."

3 Marta said, "All right, Dad."

4 Marta's mom and dad worked until the painting was done. Then Mom said, "It looks good to me."

5 Dad said, "Me, too," so they started to clean the brushes. As they came upstairs, Marta's dad said to her mom, "I must use the telephone. Why don't you take your bath first?"

6 Mom looked out at Marta and Nicky playing in the backyard. She laughed. "They can play keep-away with the football, but they can't keep away from the mud. I think they need the first baths."

Knowing the Words

Write the story words that have these meanings.

1. part of
   a house _____
   _(Par. 1)

2. close _____
   _(Par. 1)

3. to wash off _____
   _(Par. 5)

4. top part
   of a house _____
   _(Par. 5)

5. place in
   back of a house _____
   _(Par. 6)

Circle the three words in each line that belong together.

6. upstairs   idea   house   kitchen
7. chair   table   mail   picture
8. box   brush   broom   mop
9. ran   sat   raced   chased

Reading and Thinking

1. If you paint in dusty air, how

   will the paint look? _____

   _____

2. How did Marta's mom and dad's work look when it was done?

   _____

Look at each picture and circle the sentence that goes with it.

3. Dad paints
   with a brush.

   Dad is
   brushing Nicky.

4. Joe helps
   at home.

   Joe is not
   helping.

Marta Helps at Home

Read to find out how Marta helps.

1 "This is great soup," said Marta one night at dinner. "I would like some more, please. Who made it?"

2 Mom gave Dad a warm smile and said, "Well, I put it together while your father fixed breakfast. Then he cooked it all day. Who would you say made it?"

3 Marta said, "I think the two of you did." She ate some more soup. Then after a while she said, "I know what. If I do the dishes, then everyone in the family will have helped with dinner!"

4 Marta's dad said, "That would be great. Thanks, Marta."

5 After dinner Mom and Dad went to sit in the backyard. Marta started cleaning up the kitchen and washing the dishes. Later when her dad came inside, she was still hard at work. "What, still not done?" he asked.

6 Marta said, "Almost, Dad. Here are the last things." She picked the pets' dishes out of the water and set them in the window to dry. As she let the water out, Marta said, "Now every dish in the house is clean!"

Reading and Thinking

1. Where did Mom and Dad go

   after dinner? _____

2. Marta wanted to do the dishes

   because _____

   _____.

3. Write **1, 2,** and **3** to show what
   happened first, next, and last.

   ____ Marta washed the dinner
         dishes.

   ____ Marta washed the pets'
         dishes.

   ____ Marta had dinner.

Working with Words

In each rcw, circle the two letters
in each word that make the same
sound you hear in the underlined
word.

    toy   p(oi)nt b(oy) n(oi)se

1. <u>show</u> know own throw
2. <u>see</u>   tree feet please
3. <u>found</u> down around brown
4. <u>mean</u> need near read

Circle the best word for each
sentence. Then write it in the
blank.

5. Do you like this _____?
       same   game   name

6. Mike found _____ money.
       hit   him   his

7. This is my _____ hat.
       best   nest   last

8. Marta hit the _____.
       ball   call   tell

Circle each c that stands for the
sound of s in these words.

9. once   12. piece
10. doctor   13. because
11. fence   14. come

63

Bigfoot's Lesson

Read to see if Mr. Barker knows much about dogs.

1   Mr. Barker was walking home from the pet store. He saw Marta and Lee working with Bigfoot in the park. He stood and watched.

2   "Bigfoot," Marta was saying, "this is the last hot dog. Could you please do it right?"

3   Lee said, "Bigfoot, heel." Bigfoot walked around Lee and sat by her left foot. But then he started to lean on Lee. Lee said, "No!" and pushed. But Bigfoot still leaned.

4   When the children sat down, Mr. Barker walked up and said, "Hello. May I train Bigfoot for a while?"

5   "Yes, please do," said Lee.

6   Mr. Barker stood in front of the dog and said, "Bigfoot, heel!" Bigfoot walked around to Mr. Barker's left foot. Again he started to lean.

7   Mr. Barker moved to one side. Then he pulled down on the dog's collar. Bigfoot fell over on his side and snorted. He was not hurt, but he did not like that!

8   Mr. Barker said, "Do that when he leans on you, and he will soon stop."

64

Knowing the Words

Write the story words that have these meanings.

1. push on

   _____
   (Par. 3)

2. what a dog has
   around its neck _____
   (Par. 7)

3. made a noise
   in the nose _____
   (Par. 7)

Circle the three words in each line that belong together.

4. mail   library   store   park
5. heel   sit   stay   found
6. collar   leash   tag   bird
7. move   walk   run   stay

Reading and Thinking

Look at each picture and circle the sentence that goes with it.

1. Dogs and cats do not like each other.

   The dog and cat are friends.

2. Marta likes to read books.

   Marta never reads books.

3. Why did Bigfoot snort?

   _____

   _____

4. Why do you think Mr. Barker knows a lot about dogs?

   _____

   _____

Plans for the Show

What should you do to set up a dog show?

1 Marta's friends met at her house one day to make plans for the dog show.

2 Mike said, "The first thing we need to do is make our signs. Can we do that today?"

3 Marta's mother came into the room to work on the signs with the children. First she helped them write on a clean piece of paper. Then she colored some dogs at the top. "Now," she said, "you need to make your copies. Then you can put them up at school and in some stores."

4 Lee said, "Dad can take me to the library tonight. I will buy the copies, and we can put them up tomorrow."

5 Marta said, "We'll need other things for the show, too. We need enough rope to make a fence around the ring."

6 "And number signs for everyone in the show," Allen said.

7 "We'll need ribbons and prizes, too!" said Christy.

8 "It will take a lot of work. But I can tell it's going to be a great show," said Marta.

Reading and Thinking

1. This story is mostly about

____ the prize ribbons.

____ going to the library.

____ the dog show.

2. What five things do the children need for their dog show?

_____

_____

_____

_____

_____

3. Who will make the copies?

_____

Working with Words

Circle the right letters for each sentence. Then write them in the blank.

1. Do you w_____k hard?

      ar   or   ir

2. It is your t_____n to play.

      ar   or   ur

3. The dog sn_____ts loudly.

      er   or   ar

Circle the best word for each sentence. Then write it in the blank.

4. Can you make your _____?

      bag   bed   big

5. Mike wrote a _____.

      listen   last   letter

6. We filled the _____ with milk.

      pan   pet   pop

Use the underlined words to make a new word to finish each sentence.

7. Corn that can pop when you

cook it is _____.

8. A walk that is by the side of

the street is a _____.

Dad's Plans

What sometimes happens when you talk to someone who is working?

1 That night while Marta was brushing Nicky, she asked, "Dad, what should we give for prizes? Do you have any good ideas?"

2 Mom started to quiet Marta, but Dad had looked up from his work at the kitchen table. "I couldn't hear you. What did you say?"

3 Marta said, "What do you think we should give for prizes?"

4 "Oh, for your dog show. Well, blue ribbons would be nice. Look, Marta, I really need to have this work done by the time my airplane goes in the morning. We'll talk before you go to bed, all right? I should be done then."

5 "Sure, Dad, I'll be quiet," Marta said as she took Nicky outside. She sat on the steps and brushed Nicky for a short time. Then a terrible thought came to her. She called into the kitchen, "Dad, do you have to go away the day of the show?"

6 "Marta, I asked you . . . ," Dad answered. Then he said, "No, Marta. I will be right here that day. I would not miss your dog show."

68

Reading and Thinking

1. Why did Marta ask if Dad had to go away the day of the show?

_____

_____

_____

Fill in the blanks.

2. Mom and Dad talked as they painted.
They stands for

_____.

3. Marta's dad answered, and he said, "No, Marta."

_He_ stands for _____.

Working with Words

The missing word in each sentence sounds like _new._ Change the _n_ in _new_ to _bl, fl,_ and _thr._ Write the new words, and put them in the right sentences.

1. _____ _____ _____

2. The wind _____ hard.

3. I _____ my dog a ball.

4. The bird _____ away.

Circle the best word for each sentence. Then write it in the blank.

5. Marta will _____ Nicky.

grass   brush   growl

6. Will Dad _____ to be here?

dry   play   try

The ending **-er** means "more" and the ending **-est** means "most." Add the endings **-er** and **-est** to these base words.

	-er	**-est**
clean	_cleaner_	_cleanest_
7. kind	_____	_____
8. fast	_____	_____

69

Helping Friends

How can Marta and Mrs. Peters help each other?

1   Marta was watering the grass. She saw Mike's grandmother out in the yard working in her flowers. Mrs. Peters would cut a flower. Then she would bend down to put it into a basket at her feet.

2   She looked tired when she put her hands to her back and stood up. Mrs. Peters saw Marta and waved. Then she called, "Hello, Marta, how are you today?"

3   "I'm fine, Mrs. Peters. May I hold that basket for you?"

4   "Why, yes, Marta. How kind of you."

5   As they worked, Marta said, "Your flowers are beautiful this year."

6   "Thank you, Marta. I've worked hard at keeping the weeds out." Mrs. Peters then asked, "Is everything ready for your dog show?"

7   Marta was glad she had asked. "Well, almost everything. Do you know where we can get some blue ribbons that don't cost much?"

8   Mrs. Peters said, "Why, yes, I think I could make them if everyone helped me. That won't cost much!" Marta and Mrs. Peters looked at each other and smiled.

Reading and Thinking

Put each word in the right blank.

entered   glitter   prizes

1. This _____ will make the ribbon shiny.

2. Lee _____ her dog in the show.

3. We will give ribbons for

   _____.

4. How did Mike and Marta get a

   can full of money? _____

   _____

   _____

Working with Words

Sometimes the letter c stands for the sound s makes as in *city*. Circle each c that stands for the sound of s in these words.

1. circle   3. city
2. cat   4. car

Circle the best word for each sentence. Then write it in the blank.

5. I know _____ you want.
   what   shut   that

6. I'll be _____ in a minute.
   chair   there   where

7. The _____ blew hard.
   will   well   wind

8. Please _____ my dish.
   fall   fell   fill

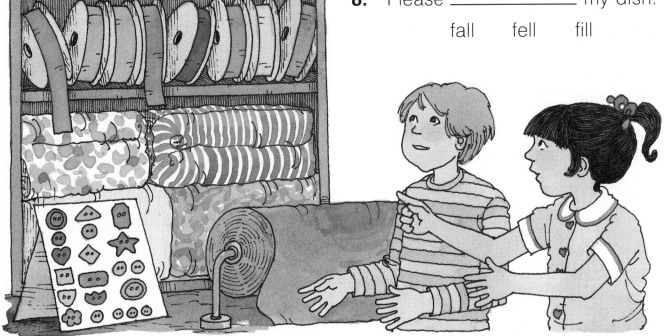

Mom Helps the Show

How does Marta's mom help?

1 The next day at the park, Mike and Joe got four more people signed up. The boys took the money they got to Marta's house. Marta's mother said, "Good work. I'll put this away for now. Do you know if Marta got permission from the city to use the park for this show?"

2 With big eyes, Mike said, "No."

3 Joe said, "We didn't even think of that."

4 Marta's mom nodded and said, "Well, I will look into it. Don't say a thing about it for a while.

5 But Mike and Joe couldn't help looking at each other while they helped Marta and Mrs. Peters with the ribbons. Marta and Mrs. Peters were hard at work and didn't even see the looks.

6 Mrs. Peters made a big "5" in paste on a green ribbon. She handed it to Marta, who shook gold glitter on the paste. Marta said, "These will be the best ribbons a dog show ever had!"

7 Just then Mom came in to say, "I called and asked for permission to have the dog show at the park. They say we can use the park at no cost!"

Reading and Thinking

Put each word in the right blank.

permission   paste   nodded

1. Marta _____ her head.

2. I have _____ to go.

3. _____ will make the ribbon stick together.

4. Who called the people who run the park? _____

5. How do you think Mike and Joe felt while they were helping with the ribbons? _____

_____

Learning to Study

Write each set of words in A-B-C order.

1. people   money   other

_____

_____

_____

2. busy   paste   cost

_____

_____

_____

3. glitter   ribbon   city

_____

_____

_____

Nicky Remembers a Friend

Read to see whom Nicky remembers.

1   Marta and Mike were in the basement working on big number signs. They were hard at work because everyone who entered a dog in the show would need a sign. Mom knocked on the door and said, "Marta, look who is here!" A bright-eyed woman walked into the room.

2   "Grandmother!" shouted Marta. She ran to give her a hug.

3   "This must be Nicky," said Marta's grandmother as she leaned over to pet Nicky's head. "You are right, Marta. She looks like a wonderful dog." Nicky was sniffing Grandmother's coat.

4   Then Marta's grandfather entered the room and said, "See who came with us, Marta." Nicky started to bark and jump up. She was trying to get past Grandmother.

5   Marta's mom said, "Nicky, what is wrong with you? Now stop that!"

6   Then a woman said, "Nicky, sit!"

7   At once Nicky sat down, and Marta said, "It's Aunt Rosa!"

8   Aunt Rosa said, "Are you surprised to see me? You should know I would not miss seeing you and Nicky in the dog show tomorrow."

Reading and Thinking

1. Who made the number signs?

   _____

2. What do you think Nicky was sniffing on Grandmother's coat?

   _____

3. Write **1, 2,** and **3** to show what happened first, next, and last.

   ____ Aunt Rosa said, "Nicky, sit!"

   ____ Grandfather talked to Marta.

   ____ Mom knocked on Marta's door.

Working with Words

In each sentence, circle the word that is made of two shorter words. Write the two words on the lines.

(Everyone) met at Lee's house.

Every   *one*

1. Do you ever play football?

   _____   _____

2. Grandmother gave Marta a hug.

   _____   _____

Circle the best word for each sentence. Then write it in the blank.

3. They played with _____ toys.

   chair   their   where

4. I am _____ in line.

   while   short   third

In each row, circle the two letters in each word that stand for the vowel sound you hear in the underlined word.

5. <u>day</u>   paint   train   stay

6. <u>each</u>   green   mean   feet

7. <u>know</u>   coat   show   own

8. <u>proud</u>   down   about   now

81

The Dog Show

Will Marta get nervous when she does something in front of a crowd?

1 After drying her hands, Marta took up Nicky's leash again. The waiting was hard for Marta. She was nervous, but Nicky was not. Nicky looked up at her and wiggled with delight. Nicky liked this crowd of people and dogs. Marta petted her and gave her a little smile. It was almost their turn.

2 She saw Lee and Bigfoot standing with Aunt Ming and Toy. Christy and Joe were there, waiting their turns in the ring. Allen was holding his puppy, Paws. He waved to Marta. "Great dog show," he called, and Marta waved back.

3 Marta's grandmother came up to her and gave her a little hug. "Try to look like this is lots of fun, Marta," she said quietly. "Don't let Nicky get nervous."

4 Everyone clapped for Mike and Flash as they walked out of the ring. Marta smiled at Mike. Then Mr. Barker, the judge, said, "Number ten, you may start."

5 Marta said, "Nicky, heel." All eyes were on them as they walked into the ring.

Write the story words that have these meanings.

1. afraid

_____
(Par. 1)

2. a number of people together

_____
(Par. 1)

3. place for a dog show

_____
(Par. 5)

Put a check by the meaning that fits the underlined word in each sentence.

4. Marta saw Lee standing there.

_____ something that cuts wood

_____ used her eyes

5. Marta walked into the ring.

_____ sound a telephone makes

_____ a circle where a show is

Put each word in the right blank.

crowd   judge   nervous

1. The _____ of people clapped.

2. Who will _____ the dog show?

3. She is _____ about the show.

4. How did Nicky feel at the dog

show? _____

_____

5. How do you think Nicky and Marta will do in the show?

_____

Gold Ribbon Winner

Who will win the gold ribbon?

1   Mr. Barker quieted everyone. He said, "We have one more prize to give. All of you now in the ring have won ribbons today. Now one of you will win a gold ribbon."

2   Gold ribbon? Marta looked in surprise at Mrs. Peters, who was holding up a gold ribbon.

3   The judge said, "All of the dogs here are well trained. I can't pick a winner. I will now ask each dog to show us a trick. When the crowd claps the most, that dog wins the gold ribbon."

4   Allen had Paws jump on two feet. Mike had Flash turn over and over. Lee rode on top of Bigfoot. Joe had his dog, Ears, stand on his back feet, and Christy had Shoes bark different ways. Other dogs did other tricks. Then, last of all, it was Marta's turn.

5   Marta was glad she had worked on a special trick with Nicky. She said, "Nicky, stay." Then Marta walked into the ring. She lay down on her back and called, "Nicky, racehorse!" All eyes were on Nicky as she ran to Marta as fast as she could. Then Nicky jumped over Marta from her head to her feet! The crowd clapped hard, and Nicky was the gold ribbon winner!

Reading and Thinking

1. Why couldn't Mr. Barker pick a winner? _____

   _____

   _____

2. What makes you think that Marta did not know about the gold ribbon?

   _____

   _____

3. Why did the crowd pick Nicky to win? _____

   _____

Working with Words

Circle the best word for each sentence. Then write it in the blank.

1. I am still _____ for Nicky.

   clapped   clapping

2. Nicky _____ over Marta.

   jumped   jumping

Add 's to these words to show what belongs to each one. Write the new word.

3. judge   _____ smile

4. Marta   _____ turn

5. Nicky   _____ ribbon

Circle g when it stands for the sound of g in go.

6. good   8. judge
7. garden   9. again

85

The Forest Story Teller

How did Uncle Bunny learn to write?

1   Bless my ears and whiskers! I'm so glad I learned to write! When I was just a young rabbit, a school was near my house. One day I saw a box under a window at the school. I climbed on top and listened. The children were learning to write.

2   "They can learn with such little ears," I said to myself. "Maybe I can learn as well with my big ears!"

3   So each day I climbed up to the window to watch and listen. At night I practiced writing in the snow.

4   "What funny tracks!" said Red Squirrel one evening.

5   "These tracks are writing," I said. "Writing uses things called letters. These letters say Red Squirrel."

6   I began with letters and short words. Soon I thought about writing some short stories.

7   Other friends came to watch. They began calling me Uncle Funny Bunny. I'm still funny, but now they just call me Uncle Bunny. They are happy that I wrote the stories in this book about them. I hope you'll be just as glad.

Knowing the Words

Write the words from the story that have these meanings.

1. face hairs _____
   (Par. 1)

2. did over and over _____
   (Par. 3)

3. did write _____
   (Par. 7)

Working with Words

Circle the right word to finish the sentence. Then write the word in the blank.

1. The team ran a good _____.
   (face, case, race)

2. Hit the ball with the _____.
   (bell, bat, bed)

Reading and Thinking

1. Check the answer that tells what the story is mostly about.

   _____ how children learn

   _____ Uncle Bunny's big ears

   _____ how Uncle Bunny learned to write

2. Look at the picture. Check the two sentences that tell about the picture.

   _____ Uncle Bunny wears glasses.

   _____ Uncle Bunny drives a car.

   _____ Uncle Bunny can write.

3. Uncle Bunny found a box under a

   _____.

Some things are real and some are make-believe. Write **R** by real things. Write **M** by make-believe things.

4. _____ Rabbits can write.

5. _____ Children can learn.

6. _____ Squirrels can talk.

Thunder and Rain

If you were a deer caught in a storm, where would you go?

1   I was eating lunch in the clover field when the sky turned very dark. Thunder rumbled all around. "Rabbits crabbits!" I thought as I ran for home. "It was going to be such a good lunch."

2   On my way through the field I saw Mrs. Whitetail and Spotty, my deer friends. I wondered why they were not hurrying home. "Mrs. Whitetail," I called, "didn't you hear the thunder?"

3   "Yes, we were under the trees when we heard it," she called back. "Spotty tried to run away. But we must stay quiet in a storm. Rain in the trees makes so much noise. We must be still and listen for danger.

4   "We'll rest here in the open field until the storm passes. Then we'll return to the trees. We may get wet, but we'll be safe."

5   "Bless my ears and whiskers!" I cried. "I don't like to get wet. I'm going home to keep dry and think about the lunch I'm missing." Oh, well, maybe the clover will be even better after the rain.

Knowing the Words

Write the words from the story that have these meanings.

1. kind of plant _____
   (Par. 1)

2. storm sound _____
   (Par. 1)

3. loud sounds _____
   (Par. 3)

The words *come* and *go* have meanings so different that they are **opposite.** Make a line from each word in the first list to the word in the second list with the opposite meaning.

4. wet   noise

5. quiet   dry

6. stay   leave

Working with Words

A word without any endings is a **base word.** The base word of *talking* is *talk.* Circle each base word below.

1. listens 2. pushed 3. eating

Sometimes one word stands for two words. The word *didn't* stands for *did not.* Write a word from the story that can stand for each pair of words.

4. we will _____
   (Par. 4)

5. I am _____
   (Par. 5)

Reading and Thinking

1. Check the answer that tells what the story is mostly about.

   _____ Uncle Bunny having lunch

   _____ where animals go during a storm

   _____ black clouds

2. Where were Mrs. Whitetail and Spotty when they heard thunder?

   _____

3. Check the sentence that tells why the deer moved to the open field.

   _____ They went there to eat.

   _____ Spotty tried to run away.

   _____ A storm was coming.

4. Why do you think Spotty tried to run away? _____

   _____

89

The Haircut

Why do you think Sniffles felt so bad about his haircut?

1   I was on my way to the carrot patch one morning when I heard a sad little voice. It sounded like my friend Sniffles.

2   The sound was like crying. I decided to see if I could help. I followed the voice and came to the pond. There was Sniffles. That little lamb was sitting by the pond. He was looking at himself in the water.

3   "What is wrong, Sniffles?" I asked. "Why are you crying?"

4   "Just look at me, Uncle Bunny!" he said. Then he cried even louder.

"I didn't know being a lamb would mean losing my wool every spring."

5   "Think about how your wool will help keep people warm," I said. "It will make coats and hats and gloves. Doesn't that make you happy?"

6   "Yes," he answered, "but I need to keep warm, too. And I look so funny without my coat."

7   "Your coat will start to grow back very soon," I said. "In the summer you will like being cool."

8   "I guess you are right, Uncle Bunny," Sniffles said. "Maybe it's just that this was my very first haircut."

90

Knowing the Words

Write the words from the story that have these meanings.

1. a small place _____
   (Par. 1)

2. hair cut from sheep _____
   (Par. 4)

3. between cold and warm _____
   (Par. 7)

Circle the three words in each row that belong together.

4. morning   year   night   afternoon

5. coats   hats   feet   shoes

6. wet   cold   warm   hot

7. happy   sad   angry   old

Learning to Study

Number the words to show A-B-C order for each list.

1. ____ lamb   2. ____ cool

   ____ carrot   ____ answered

   ____ friend   ____ patch

   ____ wool   ____ wrote

Reading and Thinking

1. Check the answer that tells what the story is mostly about.

   ____ keeping people warm

   ____ being cool in the summer

   ____ Sniffles giving his wool

2. What was Sniffles doing by the pond? _____

   _____

3. Sniffles thought he looked funny

   because _____

   _____.

Words such as *he, his, she,* and *her* take the place of other words. Read these sentences. Fill in the blanks.

4. Sniffles cried as he saw himself.

   He stands for _____.

5. Uncle Bunny ate his carrots.

   His stands for _____.

Write **R** by the real things. Write **M** by the make-believe things.

6. ____ Lambs wear gloves.

7. ____ Coats are made from wool.

91

The Tree Planter

Why do squirrels put away food?

1   One winter morning I heard lots of angry chattering. I hopped over the hill toward the noise. Red Squirrel was almost standing on his head in the snow. He was digging as fast as he was chattering. "Just let me catch that thief! I'll show that one a thing or two!"

2   Red stopped digging and looked up. He waved his tail and looked angry enough to eat a rock.

3   "Someone took my acorn! I put it under this tree last fall. Now it's gone! Sorry, Uncle Bunny, but I can't talk now. I've got work to do!"

4   Red kept digging faster and faster into the snow. At last he came up with an acorn between his front teeth. "At last," he cried, "I've found my breakfast!" Then he ran up an oak tree faster than I could say, "Bless my ears and whiskers!"

5   I laughed to myself. Red Squirrel never remembers where he hides his acorns. When spring comes, they start to grow into tiny oak trees. He plants new trees without knowing it.

Knowing the Words

Write the words from the story that have these meanings.

1. one who takes something _____
   <small>(Par. 1)</small>

2. nut from oak tree _____
   <small>(Par. 3)</small>

Check the meaning that fits the underlined word in each sentence.

3. We clean up leaves in the <u>fall.</u>

   ____ part of year before winter

   ____ to drop suddenly

4. I <u>wave</u> as I leave for school.

   ____ make a good-bye sign

   ____ rolling water

Working with Words

Write **S** beside each word that stands for one of something. Write **P** by each word that stands for more than one.

1. ____ noise   2. ____ acorns

Circle the right word to finish each sentence. Then write the word in the blank.

3. The cold wind _____

   in our faces. (threw, flew, blew)

4. The cars hit with a loud _____.
   (splash, crash, flash)

Reading and Thinking

1. Red Squirrel planted an acorn in

   what part of the year? _____

Write **T** if the sentence is true.
Write **F** if it is not true.

2. ____ Oak trees grow from acorns.

3. ____ The story happens in winter.

4. Red could not find his acorn

   because _____

   _____.

5. What do you think Red did after

   he ran up the tree? _____

   _____

6. How did Red Squirrel feel when he thought someone took his nut?

   _____

The Skunks' Present

Why wouldn't anyone want a present from a skunk?

1   On my way to the carrot patch one morning, I met Mrs. Skunk and her family. She was waving her bushy tail like a flag. Behind her were six little skunks, waving their tails, too.

2   "Hello, Mrs. Skunk," I called to her. "Would you like to have breakfast with me?"

3   "Thank you, Uncle Bunny," she said. "We are on our way to look for insects."

4   Just then I heard an angry growl behind me. I turned. A big dog was running right at us.

5   "Quick, come under this berry bush with me!" I called. "The branches will keep us safe." I rolled under the bush and waited for the skunk family. But the mother and her babies stayed where they were. Mrs. Skunk started dancing her front feet up and down. The little skunks danced, too. Suddenly Mrs. Skunk and her little ones turned their backs and waved their tails.

6   That big dog stopped so fast. Then he turned and hurried away.

7   "Rabbits crabbits," I thought to myself. "I should have guessed what would happen. Even that dog wanted to stay away from the skunk smell!"

94

Knowing the Words

Write the words from the story that have these meanings.

1. black and
white animal _____
(Par. 1)

2. small animals such
as bees and ants _____
(Par. 3)

Words that mean the same or nearly the same are called **synonyms.**
Circle two synonyms in each row.

3. begin   stop   call   start

4. bird   rabbit   skunk   bunny

5. listen   catch   see   look

6. run   car   hurry   dog

Learning to Study

Number the words to show A-B-C order for each list.

1. ____ turn

____ patch

____ bee

____ skunk

2. ____ carrot

____ growl

____ happen

____ safe

Reading and Thinking

1. Check the answer that tells what the story is mostly about.

____ how rabbits hide under berry bushes

____ a frightened dog

____ how skunks keep safe

2. Number the sentences to show what happened first, second, third, and last.

____ The skunks danced.

____ Uncle Bunny heard a growl.

____ The dog ran away.

____ Uncle Bunny met the skunks.

Write the best word to finish each sentence below.

3. We heard the band and wanted

to _____. (read, dance, believe)

4. The dog _____ at the loud noise. (growled, worked, laughed)

Make Way for Betsy

Why does Betsy like to climb trees?

1   Betsy Bear's path runs from a tall tree down to the stream. One day I found out why she has the path.

2   Betsy was climbing the tree. She pulled herself up and put one paw around the tree. She stuck her other paw into a hole in the tree. Then she pulled her paw out and licked it.

3   Suddenly I heard a buzzing sound. Bees lived inside the tree. Betsy was taking some of their honey! Angry bees buzzed around Betsy, but her fur kept her safe.

4   Before long some of the bees flew toward her face. Betsy gave a loud "Woof!" A bee gave her a sting right on her nose where she had no fur. Betsy shook her head and cried as she hurried down the tree.

5   Betsy hit the ground hard. All she could think of was her nose. She ran down the path toward the stream as bees flew after her. Splash! She jumped into the stream. The water came up around her burning nose.

6   Now I'm always careful to stay off Betsy's path. I would not want to be in the way when she needs it!

Knowing the Words

Write the words from the story that have these meanings.

1. a place to walk _____
(Par. 1)

2. insect bite _____
(Par. 4)

In each row, circle the two words with opposite meanings.

3. inside   little   claws   outside

4. long   push   hungry   pull

Working with Words

An 's at the end of a word may be used to show that something belongs to someone. Add 's to each name. Write each name in the right blank.

Uncle Bunny_____   Betsy Bear_____

1. _____ burning nose

2. _____ whiskers

Circle the right word to finish each sentence. Then write the word in the blank.

3. Please _____ your book with you. (bring, string, spring)

4. The clothes are _____.
(clean, cream, string)

Reading and Thinking

1. Where did Betsy's path go?

_____

2. What did Betsy find inside the tree? _____

3. The bees were angry because

_____.

Write **T** if the sentence is true.
Write **F** if it is not true.

4. ____ Bears and bees eat honey.

5. ____ Bears and bees make honey.

6. ____ Bees are larger than bears.

7. What do you think Betsy did when she came out of the stream?

_____

_____

A Narrow Escape

How can a rabbit trick a fox?

1 I try to keep away from Tricky and Slick Fox. Sometimes that isn't easy. Once I was hopping toward the meadow when I heard a pit-pat behind me. I hopped a little faster. The pit-pats came a little faster. When I stopped the pit-pats stopped. I looked back. There was Tricky in the middle of the path!

2 Rabbits crabbits! There wasn't much space between Tricky and me. I tossed my cane away and raced as fast as I could. I flew so fast my feet hardly touched the ground. The wind whistled past my ears. My whiskers blew against my face.

3 Then I saw something under a bush ahead. It was Slick. Tricky was chasing me to Slick's hiding place.

4 Just as Slick moved out from under the bush, I knew what to do. I closed my eyes and jumped with all my might. I sailed over Slick's head. I landed in a patch of bushes far away from the two foxes.

5 Tricky was running so fast he couldn't stop. He and Slick ran right into each other. I hopped away toward home. I guess that's one time the foxes tricked each other.

Knowing the Words

Words that mean the same or nearly the same are called **synonyms.** Use lines to match synonyms.

1. little   quick

2. close   tiny

3. fast   near

Working with Words

A **compound word** is made by putting two words together. Write a compound word for the underlined words below. One is done for you.

A word meaning <u>some</u> kind of

<u>thing</u> is *something* .

1. A time <u>after</u> the <u>noon</u> time is

_____ .

2. A <u>bird</u> whose wings make a <u>humming</u> sound is a

_____ .

Fill in each blank with the right pair of letters to make a word.

ch   sh   th   wh

3. _____iskers   6. _____ink

4. _____is   7. _____ange

5. _____eel   8. _____ort

Reading and Thinking

1. How is a hummingbird different

from most birds? _____

_____

Write **R** by the real things. Write **M** by the make-believe things.

2. _____ Hummingbirds wear glasses.

3. _____ Hummingbirds eat insects.

4. _____ Hummingbirds are different from most birds.

5. _____ Hummingbirds wear shoes.

6. Check the answer that tells what a hummingbird nest may look like.

_____ very small

_____ a box for shoes

_____ very large

Diver Hawk

How did Diver frighten Uncle Bunny?

1   Not long ago Diver Hawk frightened me. He didn't mean to, but I was scared just the same. I was resting in a field watching the sky. As I looked up I saw Diver. His wide wings were stretched out. He seemed to be floating.

2   Suddenly Diver lifted his wings over his back. He pointed his head down and began to drop. "He's seen something for lunch," I thought.

3   He dropped faster and closer. He was coming right at me! I was so scared I couldn't move. I shut my eyes. I waited. When nothing happened, I slowly opened one eye.

4   Diver was sitting on a fence nearby. "I saw you while I was floating in the sky. You were so still I just wanted to see if you were OK."

5   "I was afraid I might be your lunch," I said, feeling much better.

6   "Oh, I usually eat things that hurt farms," Diver said. "Some people don't like me, but I really help them."

7   "Bless my ears and whiskers!" I exclaimed. "I'll write a story telling how much you help!"

Knowing the Words

Write the words from the story that have these meanings.

1. scared _____
   (Par. 1)

2. closed _____
   (Par. 3)

3. cried out _____
   (Par. 7)

Circle the three words in each row that belong together.

4. wings   head   sky   beak

5. meadow   field   lake   land

6. fit   scared   frightened   afraid

Working with Words

A **compound word** is made by putting two words together. Use these words to make two compound words.

fast   light   flash   break

1. _____

2. _____

Reading and Thinking

1. Check the answer that tells what the story is mostly about.

   _____ how Diver scared Uncle Bunny

   _____ how hawks fly

   _____ animals eating lunch

2. Write two things Diver Hawk did to frighten Uncle Bunny. _____

   _____

   _____

3. Write **T** if the sentence is true. Write **F** if it is not true.

   _____ The story takes place at night.

   _____ Hawks cannot see very well.

   _____ Hawks can fly very well.

Write the best word to finish each sentence below.

4. The house was _____ after the party ended. (quiet, scared, angry)

5. My sister and her _____ took a trip. (field, friends, fence)

The Night Hunter

Read about how owls can hear.

1 With my big ears I hear very well. But not long ago I found out that size of ears isn't very important. Cynthia Owl's ears don't even show, but she hears things I can't.

2 I was in the clover field for a late supper. Suddenly I heard a long "Whoo-hoo-ee-ooo." "Who's there?" I cried.

3 "It's me, Uncle Bunny. I heard another owl. I told it to stay away."

4 I looked up and saw Cynthia Owl. She was high in a tree near the field.

"Bless my ears and whiskers!" I exclaimed. "I didn't hear anyone but you. You must have very sharp ears. They are so small I can't see them."

5 "Each of my ears is a small fold of skin. It goes from each eye down to the side of my neck," she said. "I can turn my head almost around. That way I can catch sounds from everywhere. I don't even have to move the rest of me."

6 Suddenly Cynthia flew off to the corner of the field. Soon she returned to the tree carrying a mouse.

7 Rabbits crabbits! I have good ears but not like Cynthia's. My ears don't help me find clover the way hers help find a mouse.

Knowing the Words

Write the words from the story that have these meanings.

1. how big or little
   something is _____
   (Par. 1)

2. one more _____
   (Par. 3)

3. very good, fine _____
   (Par. 4)

4. place where two
   sides come together _____
   (Par. 6)

In each row, circle the two words with opposite meanings.

5. down   off   around   up

6. tell   gone   say   came

7. show   large   small   bless

Working with Words

Circle the right word to finish each sentence. Then write the word in the blank.

1. My mother opened a _____
   of soup for lunch. (can   cane)

2. Will you _____ the gift
   for the party? (hid   hide)

3. Does your new hat _____ ?
   (fit   fight)

Reading and Thinking

1. Check the answer that tells what the story is mostly about.

   _____ Uncle Bunny's supper

   _____ how an owl uses its ears

   _____ night sounds in the forest

Write **T** if the sentence is true.
Write **F** if it is not true.

2. _____ Uncle Bunny couldn't see
   Cynthia's ears because she
   didn't have any.

3. _____ Owls hear sounds from all
   around because they turn
   their heads almost around.

4. Check the sentence that tells
   how owls and rabbits are like
   each other.

   _____ They both have ears.

   _____ They both eat carrots.

   _____ They both can fly.

Write **R** by the real things. Write **M** by the make-believe things.

5. _____ Owls can hear very well.

6. _____ Owls can hear clover grow.

7. _____ Owl ears can't be seen.

8. _____ Owls hear better than
   rabbits.

The Red Coats Are Coming

Read this story to find out about two angry friends.

1 One morning as I was hopping to the meadow, I heard angry voices. I had to find out what was wrong.

2 I hopped toward the chattering. The voices got louder and louder. Soon I found two of my forest friends. They were shouting at each other.

3 "My red coat is the prettiest in the forest!" cried Biff the redbird. "It's made of feathers and it covers almost my whole body. It is soft and very pretty. Sometimes I go to the pond just to look at myself."

4 "Soft and pretty!" answered Mrs. Coats, the ladybug. "My coat is red, too, but it is shiny and has pretty little spots on it. Not only that, my red coat helps keep me safe."

5 I sat there and watched my two friends. Suddenly I had an idea.

6 "Stop!" I cried. "I've heard enough! My red coat is the best of all! It has bright buttons. One of my pockets is big enough to hold both of you. And if my coat gets old, I can throw it away and get a new one."

7 My two friends looked at each other. "Did we really sound that silly, Uncle Bunny?" asked Mrs. Coats.

8 "Maybe we should wait for something more important to argue about," Biff added.

9 "That is a good idea," I chuckled. "Now let's go and have lunch."

Knowing the Words

Write the words from the story that have these meanings.

1. all of something _____
   _(Par. 3)

2. having great meaning _____
   _(Par. 8)

3. laughed quietly _____
   _(Par. 9)

In each row, circle the two words with opposite meanings.

4. start   right   wrong   begin
5. new   forest   trees   old
6. sound   noise   louder   quieter
7. there   here   now   time

Learning to Study

Write each group of words in A-B-C order. Each group of words will make a sentence. Use a period or a question mark to end each sentence.

1. move didn't wagon Barnie the

   _____

   _____

2. whistles new Children silver like

   _____

   _____

Reading and Thinking

1. Check the answer that tells what the story is mostly about.

   ____ Biff's soft red feathers

   ____ friends arguing about things that are not really important

   ____ how Uncle Bunny gets a new red coat

Words such as *he, she,* and *it* take the place of other words. Read these sentences. Then fill in the blanks.

2. Biff smiled as he talked.

   He stands for _____.

3. Mrs. Coats sang as she worked.

   She stands for _____.

4. My coat is red, but it is shiny.

   It stands for _____.

113

Too Late for Supper

Why did Uncle Bunny miss supper?

1   Sometimes I take a nap in the afternoon. I like to rest in the meadow where the sun is warm. I can count on Gordy Goldfinch to wake me for supper. Most times I have no trouble hearing him. But one time I slept right through his song.

2   That day my ears hurt. I had put cotton in them to keep them warm.

Then I hopped to the meadow to rest by the fence. Soon I was sound asleep. As I slept, I dreamed about the carrots I would have for supper.

3   Just before dark, Gordy flew to the meadow. He took his place on the fence as he always does. "Cheer-eee-ooo, cheer-eee-ooo, it's supper time for you," he sang.

4   I couldn't hear him. My ears were full of cotton. Gordy sang another song. Still I didn't move. The sun went down and I was still asleep. Gordy hopped down onto my head. Then he saw the cotton in my ears. He started pulling at the cotton.

5   "Rabbits crabbits!" I cried. "Who is wiggling my ears?"

6   "It's me, Uncle Bunny," Gordy answered. "I tried to wake you. I'm afraid you missed eating."

7   "Oh no, I haven't," I cried as I jumped up. "I may be too late for supper, but it's never too early for breakfast!"

Knowing the Words

Check the meaning that fits the underlined word in each sentence.

1. Uncle Bunny likes to take a <u>rest</u> in the afternoon.

    _____ that which is left

    _____ time without work

2. The sun went down and I was <u>still</u> asleep.

    _____ quiet

    _____ up to this time

Working with Words

A word part that can be said by itself is called a **syllable.** Some words have two consonants between two vowels. These words can be divided between the consonants, as in *pic/nic*. In each word below, draw a line to divide the word into syllables.

1. c o t t o n
2. a l w a y s
3. w i n d o w
4. a l m o s t
5. m o n k e y
6. s i l l y
7. c h i m n e y
8. e n g i n e

Reading and Thinking

1. Check the answer that tells what the story is mostly about.

    _____ how Uncle Bunny hurt his ear

    _____ how Uncle Bunny slept through supper

    _____ Gordy's loud, clear singing voice

2. Check the two words that tell about Gordy.

    _____ friendly   _____ mean

    _____ tired   _____ helping

Write the best word to finish each sentence below.

3. The _____ needs to be painted again. (cotton, fence, word)

4. The new road is _____ and even. (wide, green, late)

5. The _____ made us feel much better. (dirt, engine, nap)

The Insect Eater

Who helps Uncle Bunny get some sleep?

1   Sometimes Brown Bat frightens people, but she really is a good friend.

2   One night I was asleep under a berry bush. Something brushed against my nose. When I tried to go back to sleep, it went zzz-zz-zzz in my ear. I wiggled my ear and turned over. I was almost asleep again when it bit my other ear.

3   This time I was wide awake and very angry. I thought to myself, "If that insect bothers me again, I'll be ready!" I lay down again and closed my eyes. I held my cane in one paw.

4   Soon I heard the buzz again. I got my cane ready. The sound got louder and louder. Whoosh! Something with wings and tiny sharp teeth flew past my face. The teeth closed. The zzz-zz-zzz was gone!

5   "Now you'll be able to sleep, Uncle Bunny," a voice said. The insect eater landed on a branch over my head. It hung upside down and folded its wings. It was Brown Bat.

6   "Thank you, Brown Bat," I said. "Could I give you some carrots as a thank you?"

7   "Thank you, Uncle Bunny," she said, "But I just eat insects. I was happy to help. Now have a good sleep!"

116

Knowing the Words

Write the words from the story that have these meanings.

1. touched lightly _____
   (Par. 2)

2. makes angry _____
   (Par. 3)

Check the meaning that fits the underlined word in each sentence.

3. Something with wings and tiny teeth flew past my face.

   ____ by

   ____ some time before

4. Uncle Bunny lost his cane.

   ____ plant for making sugar

   ____ stick for walking

Working with Words

Write a word from the story that can stand for each pair of words.

1. I will _____
   (Par. 3)

2. you will _____
   (Par. 5)

An 's shows that a thing belongs to someone. Change these words to show what belongs to someone.

3. bat _____ wings

4. Barnie _____ tail

Reading and Thinking

1. What animals were in the story?

   _____

   _____

2. What did the insect bite?

   _____

3. Brown Bat didn't want any

   carrots because _____

   _____.

Write **T** if the sentence is true.
Write **F** if it is not true.

4. ____ Uncle Bunny thinks bats are animals that help.

5. ____ Brown Bat eats apples.

6. ____ Uncle Bunny likes all insects.

117

Whistler Digs a Home

Would you like to live underground?

1   Whistler Woodchuck lives under the ground in a long tunnel. The front door is a hole. A large rock hides it. Whistler's living room is an open space in the tunnel. The tunnel has back doors and secret paths, too.

2   He is always working to make his house better. One day I heard digging and scratching under the large rock.

3   "What does he do with all the dirt?" I thought. I looked in his front door, but I couldn't see anything. The sounds were coming closer. I sat near the front door to wait for Whistler.

4   The minutes passed, but Whistler was still under the ground. I looked into the tunnel again. All at once a stream of dirt came flying out the door. My mouth, nose, and eyes were all filled with it.

5   "Bless my ears and—achoo!" I sneezed so hard I fell over onto my back. I sat up, wiped my face, and shook my ears. Then I saw Whistler.

6   He was backing out of his hole. He was still kicking dirt wildly behind him. That's when I learned how Whistler took the dirt out of his house. The next time I won't wait so close to the door.

118

Knowing the Words

Write the words from the story that have these meanings.

1. an open path
   under the ground _____
   <small>(Par. 1)</small>

2. something only
   a few know _____
   <small>(Par. 1)</small>

3. Check the meaning that fits the underlined word in the sentence.

   I sneezed so <u>hard</u> I fell over.

   _____ not easy to do

   _____ not soft

Learning to Study

To put words in A-B-C order you must first look at the first letter of each word. If the first letters are the same, look at the second letters. Number each list to show A-B-C order.

1. _____ nose   2. _____ sound

   _____ eyes   _____ sneezed

   _____ mouth   _____ stream

   _____ face   _____ scratch

Reading and Thinking

1. Check the answer that tells what the story is mostly about.

   _____ finding the secret tunnel

   _____ Uncle Bunny's dirty face

   _____ Whistler digging a tunnel

2. Number the sentences to show what happened first, second, third, and last.

   _____ Uncle Bunny heard digging and scratching.

   _____ Uncle Bunny got his face full of dirt.

   _____ Uncle Bunny sat down to wait for Whistler.

   _____ Uncle Bunny fell over onto his back.

Write **T** if the sentence is true.
Write **F** if it is not true.

3. _____ A woodchuck's home is dark.

4. _____ A woodchuck needs strong paws.

5. What do you think Uncle Bunny will do the next time he sees Whistler digging a tunnel?

_____

119

A Hard Day's Work

Read about a small worker who is very strong.

1   "Hello, Uncle Bunny," a tired voice said to me one morning. I was on my way to the carrot patch for a quick breakfast. I looked around, but I didn't see anyone.

2   "Down here, Uncle Bunny," the voice went on. "I'm down here!" I looked toward the sound. There wasn't anyone in sight. "Please don't step on me," the little voice called.

3   I looked again. This time I saw a small seed moving across the path. But a seed had never talked to me.

4   I stretched out on the ground to get a closer look. That's when I found the answer. The talking seed was really Cookie Ant. Cookie is so tiny that the seed covered his whole body.

5   "Cookie!" I exclaimed. "That seed is ten times bigger than you are! How can you carry it?"

6   "It's hard work, Uncle Bunny," he replied. "But lots of ants carry even bigger things. We all work to keep our little ant town going. Some of us find food. Some of us take care of our home. Some of us do other things to help."

7   "Bless my ears and whiskers!" I exclaimed. "That sounds like a good idea. Maybe rabbits should start living like ants."

Knowing the Words

Write the words from the story that have these meanings.

1. reached across _____
   (Par. 4)

2. small insects _____
   (Par. 6)

Words that mean the same or nearly the same are called **synonyms.** Circle two synonyms in each row.

3. body   tiny   small   seed

4. toward   sound   away   noise

5. begin   read   answers   start

Working with Words

Write the best word to finish each sentence below.

1. I _____ the answer. (wrote, rope, rode)

2. You took the _____ street. (rock, rest, wrong)

When **un-** is added to a word, it changes the meaning of the word. The word part **un-** means "not." *Unreal* means "not real." Add **un-** to these words to finish the sentences.

3. She was ____hurt in the fall.

4. The food was ____touched.

Reading and Thinking

1. Check the answer that tells what the story is mostly about.

   ____ Uncle Bunny learning about how ants work

   ____ seeds that walk and talk at the same time

   ____ how Cookie Ant became so strong

2. How big was the seed that

   Cookie was carrying? _____

   _____

3. How was Cookie helping the ant

   town? _____

   _____

Write the best word to finish each sentence below.

4. The train went through the

   _____ under the river. (mud, tunnel, water)

5. I _____ my hair before I left for school. (brushed, learned, practiced)

6. Take the dishes _____ the kitchen. (under, above, into)

Chomper's Treasure

What could a chipmunk do with a big ear of corn?

1   One day last fall I was crossing a field. Suddenly a brown streak with white and black stripes hurried between my legs. "Bless my ears and whiskers!" I cried. "I've never seen lightning with stripes before!"

2   The streak came to a stop on the road. I saw that it was really Chomper Chipmunk. He had stopped beside an ear of corn bigger than he was.

3   "Look what I found, Uncle Bunny!" Chomper cried. "I've got to carry it away before the crows find it."

4   He bit the pieces of corn off the ear one by one. Then he filled his cheeks with the corn. Chomper's face got fatter and fatter until it was the widest part of his body. When there was no more room in his cheeks, he hurried away. He dropped into his house through a small hole under a rock.

5   Soon Chomper ran back to the corn. He filled his cheeks again and ran off. He made the same trip again and again until all the corn was gone.

6   "Chomper," I said, "you put away a lot of corn. You sleep most of the winter. Why do you need so much food?"

7   "I do sleep a lot," he answered. "But my dreams make me very hungry before spring!"

Knowing the Words

Write the words from the story that have these meanings.

1. sides of the face under the eyes _____
   (Par. 4)

2. wanting food _____
   (Par. 7)

Circle the three words in each row that belong together.

3. nap   dream   sight   sleep

4. fly   chipmunk   mouse   squirrel

5. ran   hurried   scampered   sat

Working with Words

Write the best word to finish each sentence below.

1. Do you _____ the new teacher? (know, nose, noise)

2. Did someone _____ on the door? (nest, lock, knock)

Write these compound words beside their meanings.

   underground   sunset   afternoon

3. when sun goes down _____

4. later than noon _____

5. under the ground _____

Reading and Thinking

1. What color were Chomper's

   stripes? _____

2. Check two sentences that show Chomper was smaller than Uncle Bunny.

   ____ Chomper ran between Uncle Bunny's legs.

   ____ The ear of corn was bigger than Chomper.

   ____ Chomper's cheeks got very fat.

3. How are crows like chipmunks?

   _____

Write **R** by the real things. Write **M** by the make-believe things.

4. ____ Lightning had lunch with Uncle Bunny.

5. ____ Chipmunks put away food for the winter.

6. ____ Chipmunks can carry lots of food in their cheeks.

A Place to Hide

Animals have different ways to keep safe. Read to find out what the bobwhites do to keep safe.

1   "How is the biggest family in the meadow?" I called. The Bobwhites had all their children out in the field that evening.

2   "We're fine, Uncle Bunny," Mr. Bobwhite said. "Would you like to join us? We are having our evening hiding lessons."

3   "Thank you, Mr. Bobwhite," I said. "That sounds like fun!" Soon I found an open place to watch the babies. They looked like balls of fuzz with legs.

4   "Now children," Mrs. Bobwhite said. "Pretend a hawk is near and you need to hide." At once all the bobwhites were gone.

5   "Ah-bob-white!" Mrs. Bobwhite called. Babies came from their hiding places like magic.

6   "It's time for bed," said Mr. Bobwhite. "Let's make our sleeping circle." The birds moved close to him while Mrs. Bobwhite counted heads.

7   "Oh dear," she said, "there are only fifteen. Where's Peter?"

8   "I'm over here!" a little voice said. The voice came from my coat.

9   I pulled my paw out of my pocket. A little head popped out. "Bless my ears and whiskers!" I said. "Peter found the best hiding place of all!"

124

Knowing the Words

Write the words from the story that have these meanings.

1. things to learn _____
   (Par. 2)

2. play make-believe _____
   (Par. 4)

3. made a short,
   quick move
   or sound _____
   (Par. 9)

Circle the three words in each row that belong together.

4. watch   look   hide   see

5. hawk   deer   bobwhite   crow

Working with Words

In each sentence, circle three words with the same vowel sound as the word in dark print.

1. **now**   The cow found the sweet grass and gave a loud MOO!

2. **now**   How can I drive around the mountain?

Reading and Thinking

1. Check the answer that tells what the story is mostly about.

   _____ a circle of sleeping birds

   _____ hiding lessons for the bobwhite babies

   _____ counting bobwhite babies

2. How many babies do Mr. and Mrs. Bobwhite have? _____

3. What did the bobwhite babies pretend? _____

   _____

Write **T** if the sentence is true.
Write **F** if it is not true.

4. _____ Bobwhites sleep in trees.

5. _____ Uncle Bunny's coat talks.

6. _____ Bobwhites are afraid of hawks.

7. Check two words that tell about Peter Bobwhite.

   _____ large

   _____ fuzzy

   _____ clever

125

Bumbles Finds a Friend

What does it mean to be a friend?

1 I had just found a cool place for my nap. I put one paw over my eyes and thought about a spring clover field. But I couldn't go to sleep.

2 Somewhere close by someone was crying. I waited a few minutes, but the cries just got louder.

3 "Bless my ears and whiskers! I can't sleep with this noise," I thought. So I got up, brushed my whiskers, and went to see about it.

4 I found Bumbles with big tears running down his face. "Oh, Uncle Bunny, I'm so unhappy. I can't do anything right! I'm always breaking things or running into someone. No one will even come close to me!"

5 Bumbles sneezed. His head flew up and knocked my glasses off. "See what I mean?" he cried.

6 Prickles came walking by. She saw Bumbles crying and stopped. "I don't have any friends," Bumbles said to Prickles. "I'm so unhappy!"

7 "Look at me, Bumbles," Prickles said. "I have these sharp things all over me. Nobody wants to get very close to me either. Maybe we can help each other."

8 "Uncle Bunny," Bumbles said, "I'm starting to feel better now. I'd like you to meet my new friend Prickles."

Knowing the Words

In each row, circle two words that have opposite meanings.

1. see   close   far   look

2. never   few   always   some

3. cry   break   sleep   wake

Working with Words

A word part that can be said by itself is called a **syllable.** Some words have two consonants between two vowels. These words can be divided between the consonants, as in *pic/nic.* In each word below, draw a line to divide the word into syllables.

1. h a p p y   3. w o n d e r

2. w h i s p e r   4. t r a c t o r

Walk and *talk* are **rhyming words.** In rhyming words, only the beginning sound is different. Write words that rhyme with *spring* by changing *spr* in *spring* to *r* or *w.*

5. _____   6. _____

Then use each new word in the right sentence.

7. The bird hurt its _____.

8. Will the school bell _____ ?

Reading and Thinking

1. Check the answer that tells what the story is mostly about.

   _____ Uncle Bunny's glasses

   _____ sleeping with noise

   _____ finding a friend

Write the best word to finish each sentence below.

2. If you _____ the toy, you must fix it. (jump, break, cry)

3. The _____ of the train kept us awake. (noise, rain, floating)

4. Move _____ to the front so you can see better. (later, closer, wider)

Read these sentences. Then fill in the blanks.

5. Bumbles sneezed as he cried.

   He stands for _____.

6. Prickles saw me as she walked by.

   She stands for _____.

7. The cane slipped as it hit the ice.

   It stands for _____.

A Road for Mice

Why do you think Chubby Meadow Mouse would want a straight road?

1 One morning I was hopping through the meadow. I caught my toe on a stone and hit the ground. "Rabbits crabbits!" I shouted as I pulled myself to my knees. "Stone, why don't you keep out of the way?"

2 Just then I heard tiny footsteps coming toward me. I looked up. There was Chubby Meadow Mouse looking right at me.

3 "You fell so hard, Uncle Bunny," he said. "The ground shook! Are you hurt?"

4 "My bones are shaken and my fur is dirty," I answered, "but I'm all right. That stone tripped me!"

5 "We have been trying to move that stone for a very long time," Chubby said. "We had to build our road around it. Maybe we can push it out of the way now."

6 We pushed and pulled with all our might. First the stone wiggled one way, then the other way. At last it rolled away into the grass.

7 "Thank you, Uncle Bunny," Chubby said. "Now we can make our road straight. We don't like to slow down for curves in the road when we are being chased!"

8 "I am happy to help," I said. "Maybe some day you can help me build a road straight to the clover field!"

Knowing the Words

Write the words from the story that have these meanings.

1. a present _____
   (Par. 3)

2. with nothing wrong _____
   (Par. 8)

Working with Words

Circle the right word to finish each sentence. Then write the word in the blank.

1. The snow is always _____.
   (cold   fold)

2. He got a new milk _____.
   (cut   cup)

When a word ends in *e,* the *e* may be dropped before adding **-ed** or **-ing.** Add **-ing** to these words. Then use the new words in the sentences below. One is done for you.

bounce + ing *bouncing*

3. leave + ing _____

4. He is _____ the cane beside the tree.

5. I am _____ a ball up and down.

Reading and Thinking

1. Check the answer that tells what the story is mostly about.

   _____ finding the right gift

   _____ standing on hills or rocks

   _____ Uncle Bunny's nap

Write the best word to finish each sentence.

2. The right gift will make someone

   very _____.
   (happy, lost, flat)

3. Please _____ the grass.
   (read, open, cut)

4. Check the group of words that tells about Glenda.

   _____ a very good singer

   _____ thinking of others

   _____ not a good friend

Molly Gets a Scare

Have you ever learned a lesson from being scared?

1 One day at the stream I saw my friend Donna Duck. She was giving swimming lessons to her little ducks. Five little ducks followed close behind her. Donna called, "Right foot first, then left foot. Try not to splash. Paddle smoothly, and wiggle your tail once in a while."

2 "Hi, Uncle Bunny," Donna called. She and her duck parade swam past.

3 "Hello, ducks," I answered. All the ducks waved to me in turn as they swam by me.

4 "Hi, Uncle Furry Ears!" a voice called. Far behind was the last little duck. It was Molly, splashing and throwing water everywhere.

5 "Molly," Donna cried, "his name is Uncle Bunny! Now stop being silly and catch up with us!"

6 Molly caught up. The little duck parade went on. But soon Molly was off again, this time after a flower.

7 "Maybe I can help," I said to Donna. I sat down behind a bush to wait for Molly. "Oogly-boogly, rabbits crabbits!" I shouted in my loudest voice.

8 "Help! Help!" Molly cried as she splashed toward Donna. I guess that scare was enough for Molly. Now she's always first in the duck parade!

Knowing the Words

Words that mean the same or nearly the same are called **synonyms.** In each row below, circle the two words that are synonyms.

1. closer   in   out   nearer

2. fly   see   look   sky

In each row, circle the two words with opposite meanings.

3. came   slowly   quickly   saw

4. always   sometimes   many   few

5. yes   no   things   always

Working with Words

Write the best word to finish each sentence below.

1. Angel likes to _____.
(fly, try, cry)

2. _____ is the best part of the year. (Spring, Thing, String)

Fill in each blank with the right pair of letters to make a word.

ar   or   ur

3. The little bunny grew l____ge.

4. I ate this m____ning.

5. We t____ned the page to read.

Reading and Thinking

1. Put a check by two words that tell about Angel Butterfly.

____ happy   ____ crawling

____ angry   ____ flying

2. Look at the picture. Check the two sentences that tell about it.

____ Uncle Bunny is eating the carrot.

____ Uncle Bunny ate the carrot.

____ Angel is flying.

Write the best word to finish each sentence.

3. The small plant _____ larger. (moved, came, grew)

4. My coat keeps me _____.
(little, warm, friendly)

Nibbler Makes a Mistake

Find out about Nibbler's mistake and what he can do to fix it.

1   Bonnie Beaver and her grandson Nibbler live in the stream. They have a house made of sticks and mud. Bonnie made a dam to hold back the water and to make a safe place for her family.

2   One day I heard Bonnie talking to Nibbler. "Don't forget," she said, "trees have leaves, but fence posts don't. Don't chew on any more fence posts. Cut down a little tree. We can use it to fix our house."

3   I leaned back on my cane to watch. Bonnie sat up on her back legs. She started to work on a tree with her sharp teeth. She took big bites until she had made a deep cut on one side. I watched and waited for the tree to fall.

4   Crack! Something broke, but not the tree! I felt myself falling. Then I hit the ground. Nibbler had cut down my cane! He thought it was a small tree.

5   "Oh, Uncle Bunny, I'm very sorry!" Nibbler said. "I thought your ears were the leaves."

6   Just then Bonnie's tree fell across the stream. "I've got an idea, Uncle Bunny!" Nibbler shouted. "I'll make you a new cane from that tree."

7   Now each time I use my beautiful new cane I think of the day Nibbler made a mistake.

Knowing the Words

Write the words from the story that have these meanings.

1. wall to hold
   back water _____
   (Par. 1)

2. something
   done wrong _____
   (Par. 7)

Working with Words

Write the best word to finish each sentence below.

1. Storms can bring _____.
   (rain, ran, run)

2. Can you _____ the new word?
   (said, sad, say)

3. I _____ the answer.
   (now, know, not)

An 's at the end of a word shows that a thing belongs to someone or something. Change these groups of words by using 's.

4. the branch of the tree

   the _____ branch

5. the home of Bonnie

   _____ home

Reading and Thinking

1. What did Bonnie Beaver build in the stream near her home?

   _____

2. Check the answer that tells what the story is mostly about.

   ____ how beavers chew on fence posts

   ____ beavers cutting down trees

   ____ how to build a dam

3. Check two sentences that tell how Bonnie could use the tree she cut.

   ____ She could use the branches to fix her house.

   ____ She could use the tree for fence posts.

   ____ She could use the tree to make the dam stronger.

4. Check two words about Nibbler.

   ____ sorry   ____ angry

   ____ mixed-up   ____ excited

The Shortcut

How might Uncle Bunny get across the pond?

1   For some reason carrots just didn't sound good to me one morning. Clover seemed like a much better breakfast. Not long ago I had seen some fresh, new clover across the pond. I could almost taste the clover as I thought about it.

2   Just then Sal Swan sailed along. She was looking for water plants. "Good morning, Sal," I said. "Who is your little friend?" Sal had one of her babies riding on her wide back.

3   "Hello, Uncle Bunny," Sal answered. "This is Sandy."

4   "What a fine way to look for your breakfast!" I said. Sandy just looked back at me and smiled.

5   "What are you doing here, Uncle Bunny?" Sal asked. "I thought you would be at the carrot patch."

6   "This morning I just didn't feel like eating carrots," I said. "I can't help thinking about the new clover field across the pond."

7   "Would you like a ride?" Sal asked. "That is, if you don't mind a friend." So I climbed on Sal's back and had a quick trip across the pond.

8   "I'm afraid you'll have to walk back, Uncle Bunny," Sal said. "By then you'll have a breakfast of fresh clover."

Reading and Thinking

1. Check the answer that tells what the story is mostly about.

    _____ how swans swim

    _____ how Uncle Bunny goes across the pond

    _____ eating carrots for breakfast

Read these sentences. Then fill in the blanks.

2. Sandy wiggled as she cleaned her feathers.

    She stands for _____.

3. The clover leaned as it grew.

    _It_ stands for _____.

4. Sal swam as she washed.

    She stands for _____.

Working with Words

Write the best word to finish each sentence below.

1. I have a _____ on my dress. (pen, pine, pin)

2. Can you _____ the horse? (ride, red, roll)

3. That book is _____. (win, mine, men)

4. Will you feed the _____? (can, car, cat)

5. The boys _____ their lunch. (cook, look, book)

When **re-** is added to a word, it changes the meaning of the word. The word part **re-** means "again." _Refill_ means "fill again." Add **re-** to these words to finish the sentences.

6. I will _____build the house.

7. Who will _____do these papers?

8. Please _____fill the tall jar.

9. Did you _____write the test?

10. Did the station _____run the show?

11. Please _____tell the story.

Sunny to the Rescue

Read about how Sunny helps Uncle Bunny.

1   Today was the day to comb my whiskers. I hopped to a quiet pool near the edge of the stream. The water was very still. I could see my face looking back at me.

2   I pulled a small branch from a pine tree to use as a comb. Then I leaned over the water. A streak of colors flashed before my eyes. "Bless my ears and whiskers!" I cried, leaning over a little farther.

3   All at once something splashed into the water. Then everything looked fuzzy. My glasses had fallen off my nose. They were resting on the bottom of the stream!

4   Then I heard a voice from under the water. "Who is dropping things into my home? I'm trying to keep eggs safe."

5   "I'm sorry to bother you," I said. "I dropped my glasses."

6   "Oh, it's you, Uncle Bunny," Sunny Sunfish said as he swam toward me. "The water isn't deep here. If you reach down, I think I can move your glasses into your paw."

7   I dipped both paws into the water. Sunny pushed with his nose, and soon I was holding my glasses. "Thank you, Sunny," I said. "From now on I'll comb my whiskers over a puddle!"

Write a compound word for the underlined words in each sentence.

1. A <u>storm</u> that brings <u>snow</u> is a

    _____.

2. A game with a <u>ball</u> and <u>basket</u> is

    _____.

Write the best word to finish each sentence below.

3. Be sure to look over _____ answer. (each   ears)

4. Uncle Bunny hid under a _____. (burn   bush)

5. I'll soon be in _____ grade. (word   third)

6. _____ to do your best. (Try   Fry)

1. Number the sentences to show what happened first, second, third, and last.

    _____ Uncle Bunny's glasses fell.

    _____ Sunny found the glasses.

    _____ Sunny pushed the glasses.

    _____ Uncle Bunny hopped to the pool.

Write the best word to finish each sentence.

2. The child took the _____ puppy for a walk. (deep, little, clover)

3. Can you see your _____ in the glass? (family, idea, face)

Look at the picture with the story. Write the best word to finish each sentence about the picture.

4. There is a _____ in the pool. (school, log, cage)

5. _____ are growing at the bottom of the pool. (Flowers, Rabbits, Plants)

6. The water is _____. (dirty, clean, moving)

A New Face at the Pond

How do you think Uncle Bunny might welcome someone new?

1   One evening I was going to the clover field across the pond. Someone I had not seen before was out on the water. The visitor looked like Sal Swan, but she had colored feathers. This bird was mostly gray and brown with some white. She had a long black neck and head. She looked a little like Donna Duck, but she was much larger.

2   I hopped around the pond. She came closer to me. "Hello," I said. "My name is Uncle Bunny. I don't think I've seen you here before."

3   "I'm happy to meet you, Uncle Bunny," she said. "I'm Greta Goose. Some friends and I are on our way back to our summer home."

4   "You mean you live in different places in summer and winter?" I asked. "That's a lot of moving!"

5   "We really like our summer home," she said. "But it gets too cold for us in the winter."

6   "Many of my friends sleep most of the winter," I said. "That keeps them safe from the cold."

7   "I don't think I would like to stay in bed all winter," Greta said. "All of us fly together and help each other. We have a lot of fun."

8   "It's good to learn how others live," I replied. "But I think I'll just stay here with my forest friends."

Knowing the Words

In each row, circle the two words with opposite meanings.

1. same   cold   cool   different

2. lake   long   short   pond

Working with Words

Walk and *talk* are **rhyming words.** In rhyming words, only the beginning sound is different. The missing words below rhyme with *shook.* Change *sh* in *shook* to *l, b, c,* and *t.* Then write each new word in the right sentence.

1. _____   3. _____

2. _____   4. _____

5. We _____ the wrong road.

6. Did you read the _____ ?

7. I can _____ dinner.

8. Did the car _____ new?

Write the best word to finish each sentence below.

9. I have not _____ her before. (send   seen)

10. We rode the _____ to school. (bone   bus)

Reading and Thinking

1. Check the answer that tells what the story is mostly about.

    _____ where Uncle Bunny is having dinner

    _____ meeting a new bird

    _____ Greta's safe trip

Read these sentences. Then fill in the blanks.

2. The stream sparkled as it splashed.

    It stands for _____ .

3. Sal swam as she talked to Uncle Bunny. *She* stands for _____ .

Write the best word to finish each sentence below.

4. The friends _____ letters at camp. (tell, write, do)

5. Some animals _____ berries. (make, buy, eat)

6. Did you _____ the milk? (stay, drink, grow)

7. What may Greta do after Uncle Bunny leaves? _____

    _____

A Slip on a Slide

Look at the picture. Why do you think Uncle Bunny is unhappy?

1 Susie Otter uses the stream as her playground. Her favorite thing is sliding in the mud. I was hopping along the bank one day when I heard a loud splash. I hurried ahead and saw Susie. She was scrambling out of the water. She shook herself. Water flew everywhere, even all over me.

2 "Oh, I'm sorry, Uncle Bunny," she said when she saw me. "I didn't know you were here. I just made a new slide. Would you like to try it?"

3 "It looks like fun, but I feel cold when I get wet," I replied. "How did you make the slide so smooth?"

4 "I had to move a lot of stones," Susie said, "and many plants and small branches. I've been working all week. There was one big rock stuck in the bank over there."

5 I hopped to the edge of her slide. I leaned over to see where the rock had been. My cane went one way and my feet went the other way. The next thing I knew I was at the bottom of Susie's slide, wet from ears to tail.

6 "Maybe we could call you Uncle Bunny Otter!" Susie laughed. "Aren't you glad you tried my new slide?"

7 "Rabbits crabbits!" I said, as the water ran down my whiskers. "I would like your slide better if it ended in the carrot patch!"

148

Knowing the Words

Circle the three words in each row that belong together.

1. water   stream   rock   pond
2. drive   slip   slide   fall
3. rocks   mud   stones   stuck
4. he   she   it   rabbit

Working with Words

Write the best word to finish each sentence below.

1. The class will _____ for the bird. (care   car)

2. Did someone _____ dinner? (barn   burn)

Most words add **-s** or **-es** to show more than one. Words that end in *y* are different. In most words that end in *y*, change the *y* to *i*, and add **-es.** Change the words below to mean more than one. One is done for you.

berry _*berries*_

3. story _____

4. penny _____

5. puppy _____

6. library _____

Reading and Thinking

1. Check the answer that tells what the story is mostly about.

_____ how Susie moved a rock from the bank

_____ Uncle Bunny's wet whiskers

_____ Susie Otter's new mud slide

2. How long did Susie work to make her slide? _____

3. Susie said she was sorry to Uncle Bunny because _____

_____.

4. Why doesn't Uncle Bunny like to get wet? _____

_____

5. Check three sentences that tell how Susie Otter is a hard worker.

_____ Susie moved one big rock from the bank.

_____ Susie moved plants and branches.

_____ Susie went down the slide.

_____ Susie shook water all over.

_____ Susie moved lots of stones to make her new slide.

Lefty's Old Suit

What do you do with clothes you can't wear anymore? Find out what one animal does.

1   The stream is one of my favorite places. It's a wonderful place for a treasure hunt. Sometimes I find a shiny stone or a pretty shell there. It's just fun to see what I can find.

2   One day I found an old suit that belonged to Lefty Crayfish. The thin shell was shaped just like Lefty. It looked as if he had been covered with ice but had crawled out of it.

3   "What could have happened to the rest of Lefty?" I thought. Then I saw his left front claw sticking out from under a rock. He had lost his right claw in a fight with another crayfish. Lefty is growing a new claw. It will soon be as big as the claw he lost, but we'll still call him Lefty.

4   "Lefty," I called, "I found the suit you lost!"

5   "Oh, I didn't lose it, Uncle Bunny," he said from under his rock. "That suit was too small. I pulled myself together and backed out of it. I'm growing a new suit, so I don't need the old one."

6   "Can you come out and show me your new suit?" I asked.

7   "My shell is still soft," Lefty answered. "It isn't safe for me to come out until it is hard."

8   "I'm glad I don't change my suit," I thought. "I would feel very strange hiding under a rock to grow new fur."

Knowing the Words

Circle two synonyms in each row.

1. glad   claw   stone   happy
2. lost   knew   rock   stone

Working with Words

The spelling of some base words is changed before an ending is added. Words such as *bat* must have the last letter doubled before adding **-ed** or **-ing.** Double the last letter and add the endings to these words to finish the sentences. One is done for you.

cut   hit   pet

(ed) The dog likes to be *petted*.

1. (ing) We are _____ the ball.

2. (ing) He is _____ the cake.

Circle the right word to finish the sentence. Then write the word in the blank.

3. Did you read the _____ ?
   (nine, sign, fine)

4. I heard what he _____.
   (said, fed, bed)

5. Please get the key to the _____.
   (cap, car, can)

Reading and Thinking

1. Check the answer that tells what the story is mostly about.

   _____ Lefty's missing claw

   _____ a crayfish's shell

   _____ a rock in the stream

2. What did Lefty's shell look like?

   _____

3. Uncle Bunny knew Lefty was

   under the rock because _____

   _____.

4. Why is Lefty called Lefty?

   _____

   _____

Write **T** if the sentence is true.
Write **F** if it is not true.

5. _____ Crayfish are always friendly with each other.

6. _____ Shells help keep crayfish safe.

7. What do you think Uncle Bunny might do with Lefty's old suit?

   _____

Tony Takes a Dive

Read the story to find out how Uncle Bunny helped Tony Turtle.

1   Near the pond one day, I almost fell over an unusual rock. It was nearly round with a flat top. The bottom was green. I hadn't seen the rock before.

2   I leaned over to get a closer look. When I was just a whisker's length away, the rock talked. "Can you help me, Uncle Bunny?" it said.

3   "Bless my ears and whiskers!" I exclaimed. I jumped back a few steps. A head and four legs slowly poked out of the rock. I bent my head over so that I was looking upside down. Then I saw that the rock was Tony Turtle.

4   "I was eating berries from a bush up on the hill," Tony said. "When I reached for a berry, my foot slipped.

I rolled down the hill and landed on my back. Now I can't turn over."

5   I tried to push Tony, but he just turned in circles on his back. I pushed with my cane and with my paws. Nothing worked. Then I shut my eyes and pushed with all my might. Tony shot over the edge of the bank, still upside down. Then he dropped into the water, where he could turn right side up. "Thanks, Uncle Bunny!" he called. "I'm all right now!"

6   "I'm glad I could help, Tony," I answered. "All that pushing made me hungry. I think I'll go look for that berry bush."

Knowing the Words

Write the words from the story that have these meanings.

1. not like
   most things _____
    (Par. 1)

2. how long
   something is _____
   (Par. 2)

Working with Words

Circle the right word to finish the sentence. Then write the word in the blank.

1. I finished _____ grade.
   (first   forest)

2. You are too _____ to
   reach the top. (sharp   short)

The letter *c* can stand for the sound of *s* as in *city* and *k* as in *cat*. Circle words that have *c* as in *city*. Cross out words that have *c* as in *cat*.

(city)   ~~cat~~

3. crawl   cent   corner   fence
4. across   place   tractor   ice
5. once   color   dance   climb
6. clown   bounce   popcorn   face
7. magic   princess   picnic   can't

Reading and Thinking

1. Number the sentences to show what happened first, second, third, and last.

   _____ Tony shot over the bank.

   _____ Tony rolled down the hill.

   _____ Tony was eating berries.

   _____ Uncle Bunny pushed Tony.

2. Where did Uncle Bunny find

   Tony? _____

3. Tony was on his back because

   _____.

4. Tony looked like a rock because

   _____.

5. Check the answer that shows Uncle Bunny got close to Tony.

   _____ Uncle Bunny wanted a
         closer look.

   _____ Uncle Bunny was a
         whisker's length away.

Fooling Mrs. Buzz

How would you act toward an angry bee? Read about Uncle Bunny and Mrs. Buzz.

1   Mrs. Buzz and I both like clover. Most times there is enough in the field for the two of us. But one day we were very grumpy about sharing.

2   I was finishing my breakfast when I found the freshest clover plant I had ever seen. I was ready to bite the fresh, pink blossom. Just then a loud, angry bee buzzed by my nose.

3   "I was here first! Leave that clover alone!" said Mrs. Buzz. She sat on the blossom that was almost in my mouth. My cheeks were so full of clover I could not answer.

4   "I'll teach you!" Mrs. Buzz cried. She flew from the blossom to my nose. Her stinger looked very sharp and long enough to reach my toes. I had to think fast!

5   "Sting my nose as much as you like, just don't sting my cane," I cried.

6   "Hum!" she buzzed. "You should not have told me that!" Then she landed on my cane. She poked her stinger down so hard the stinger bent right over. "Ouch!" Mrs. Buzz cried.

7   "Ouch, oh, ouch! My poor cane!" I cried, too, because I wanted Mrs. Buzz to think she had really hurt me. I limped away, rubbing my cane. From that day on I've always been nice to Mrs. Buzz. She may not be so easy to fool another time!

Knowing the Words

Write the words from the story that have these meanings.

1. unhappy _____
(Par. 1)

2. using together _____
(Par. 1)

3. flower _____
(Par. 2)

Working with Words

A word part that can be said by itself is called a **syllable.** Some words have two consonants between two vowels. These words can be divided between the consonants, as in *pic/nic.* Write each word below. Then draw a line to divide the word into syllables.

1. almost _____

2. blossom _____

3. rubbing _____

Circle the right word to finish each sentence. Then write the word in the blank.

4. Did you hear the _____ ?
(knew, knock, know)

5. I knew that was the _____
answer. (write, wrong, wrote)

Reading and Thinking

1. Number the sentences to show what happened first, second, third, and last.

_____ Uncle Bunny was eating.

_____ Uncle Bunny limped away.

_____ Mrs. Buzz poked her stinger down on the cane.

_____ Mrs. Buzz flew to Uncle Bunny's nose.

2. How did Uncle Bunny fool Mrs.

Buzz? _____

_____

3. Check two sentences that tell how Uncle Bunny and Mrs. Buzz were the same.

_____ They both got hurt.

_____ They both wanted clover.

_____ They were both grumpy.

The Gold Coat

Would Uncle Bunny like to have a gold coat? Why or why not?

1 Something bright and shiny caught my eye one morning as I walked by the pond. I looked closer. The shiny thing moved, but the water was very still.

2 I put my nose down to the water to get a better look. Suddenly I had a face full of water. The shiny thing splashed me! "Bless my ears and whiskers!" I exclaimed.

3 "Hello, Uncle Bunny," Gilda Goldfish said. "I didn't think you were so close to the water. I'm sorry I got you all wet!"

4 "Gilda, you look so shiny in the still water," I said. "I thought I had found some gold."

5 "Sometimes my bright, shiny coat is a problem," Gilda said. "If friends can see me, then enemies can see me, too. A green or brown coat might be better. I could hide just by being still on the bottom of the pond.'

6 "Lots of animals keep safe that way," I said. "Their coats are the color of their homes. Some animals even change color to match where they are."

7 "That sounds like a great idea," Gilda said. "When I need to hide, I must find some weeds or a rock."

8 "I'm glad my brown fur helps me hide," I said. "I wouldn't want to be Uncle Goldbunny!"

Reading and Thinking

1. Check the answer that tells what the story is mostly about.

   ____ Uncle Bunny's wet face

   ____ how animals keep safe

   ____ hiding in the weeds

Write the best word to finish each sentence.

2. Please _____ before you answer. (carry, hide, think)

3. We ran _____ the house in the rain. (toward, over, away)

Look at the picture on this page. Answer these questions about it.

4. Where is Gilda Goldfish hiding?

   _____

5. What is Sunny Sunfish wearing?

   _____

Working with Words

The ending **-y** added to a word can mean "full of." The word *rainy* means "full of rain." Write the meanings for these words. One is done for you.

dirty *full of dirt*

1. grassy _____

2. creamy _____

In rhyming words, only the beginning sound is different. In each sentence, write the word from the box that rhymes with the underlined word.

soap   bright   caught

3. Late at <u>night</u>, the stars are very

   _____.

4. I <u>hope</u> that I can find the

   _____.

5. My mother <u>bought</u> the fish that I

   _____.

Circle the right word to finish each sentence. Write the word in the blank.

6. We played, _____ we lost. (bit, bat, but)

7. Did you find your _____ ? (hit, hat, hot)

Flash Firefly

*Read to find out why Flash Firefly
didn't want to be called a fly.*

1 "Grandpa, the stars are falling!"
Sarah Jean called one night. I
couldn't see anything in the sky. And
I couldn't see Sarah Jean. Then I
found her hiding under a bush. She
was flat on the ground.

2 "Look out, here comes one now!"
she shouted. As I turned around,
Flash Firefly flew past me. He blinked
his light and landed on a branch.

3 "Pick yourself up and come out,
Sarah Jean," I chuckled. "There is
nothing to be afraid of. It's Flash
Firefly."

4 "Who is calling me a fly?" Flash
asked. "I'm a beetle and proud of it."

5 "But you're called a firefly!" Sarah
Jean called from under the bush.

6 "Names don't always mean just
what they say. Sometimes I'm called
a lightning bug, too, but I can't make
lightning," Flash said. "I would like
to stay, but my friend Blinky is
calling." Flash blinked his light and
flew away.

7 "I didn't hear anything, Grandpa,"
Sarah Jean said.

8 "That's because fireflies use their
lights the way we use words," I said.

9 "I guess the stars were not falling
at all," Sarah Jean laughed. "Flash
and Blinky were just having a little
talk!"

158

Reading and Thinking

1. Check the answer that tells what the story is mostly about.

   _____ stars falling from the sky

   _____ Uncle Bunny's walk

   _____ how Sarah Jean learns about fireflies

2. Why was Sarah Jean afraid? _____

   _____

3. How is a firefly like a fly? _____

   _____

Write **R** by the real things. Write **M** by the make-believe things.

4. _____ Stars fall to the ground.

5. _____ Fireflies make lightning.

6. _____ Fireflies are beetles.

Working with Words

Fill in each blank with the right pair of letters to make a word.

ar   er   or

1. Will you read me a st_____y?

2. We worked with flash c_____ds.

3. She took h_____ book home.

The letter g can stand for the sound of j as in cage and g as in girl. Circle words that have g as in cage. Cross out words that have g as in girl.

cage   ~~girl~~

4. glass   large   hungry   goose

5. orange   gold   tag   together

Write the compound words from the story that have these meanings.

6. thing of
   any kind _____
   (Par. 1)

7. insect that
   makes light _____
   (Par. 2)

In each sentence, circle two words with the same vowel sound as the word in dark print.

8. **soap**   Wear your coat when you walk down the road.

9. **grow**   I can throw the ball low.

159

The Champion Jumper

Who is the champion jumper? Read to find out.

1   I used to think I was the best jumper in the meadow. Now I know that isn't true. Carol Anne and I were eating in the clover field one day. "Grandpa!" she said. "Someone has been eating our clover."

2   "Rabbits crabbits!" I shouted. "Just wait until I get my paws on the one who did this!"

3   "You'll never catch the champion jumper!" a voice called. I turned around. Just then Jumper, the grasshopper, sprang over my head.

4   "Champion jumper!" I cried. "We can have a contest. That will show who is the champion jumper! If you

win, Jumper, I'll share this field with you. If I jump farther, you'll have to eat your lunch somewhere else." We both got ready.

5   I shook myself and took a deep breath. I was ready to take my best leap. Jumper shouted, "Go!" I took off and sailed far over the clover patch. I landed in the next meadow.

6   Jumper pushed herself into the air and opened her wings. She flew over my head and landed on the far side of the meadow.

7   "Well, I guess that shows I'm not the best jumper after all," I said. "We'll be sharing this field from now on. Why don't we begin by eating lunch together right now?"

Reading and Thinking

1. Uncle Bunny is Carol Anne's

_____ .

2. Who jumped first in the contest?

_____

Write **T** if the sentence is true.
Write **F** if it is not true.

3. ____ Uncle Bunny didn't think he
could win the contest.

4. ____ Uncle Bunny learned
something about himself.

5. ____ Uncle Bunny keeps his
word.

6. What do you think Uncle Bunny
and Jumper did after lunch?

_____

_____

Working with Words

Circle words that have *c* as in *city*.
Cross out words that have *c* as in *cat*.

(city)   ~~cat~~

1. picture   uncle   bounce   nice

2. popcorn   corner   face   cut

3. fence   across   candle   dance

An *'s* at the end of a word may be
used to show that something belongs
to someone. Change these groups of
words using *'s*.

4. the clover of the rabbit

the _____ clover

5. the legs that belong to Jumper

_____ legs

6. the lunch of the grasshopper

the _____ lunch

Circle the right word to finish each
sentence. Then write the word in the
blank.

7. I can't _____ of it.
(think, thank, tent)

8. She _____ into the apple.
(bat, bit, but)

161

Pokey Snail

Did you ever trip over your own feet?
Read this story about Pokey Snail.

1 One summer morning I was hopping down the path too fast. I stumbled and crashed to the ground! "Grandpa, are you hurt?" a little voice called. I picked myself up. I looked and saw Sonny stretched across the path. I had fallen over him.

2 "My bones are shaken and my fur is dirty," I replied, "but I'm all right. What are you doing?"

3 "I'm waiting for Pokey Snail to come home to his shell," Sonny said. He pointed to a shell by the path.

4 "Pokey takes his house with him," I said. "He's always at home anywhere. Pokey is inside, taking a nap." I tapped on the shell.

5 Little by little, a sleepy Pokey appeared. "I grew tired and stopped to rest. How did your fur get so dirty, Uncle Bunny?" Pokey asked.

6 "I tripped over Sonny," I said.

7 "I'm not surprised," Pokey laughed. "You rabbits have so many feet! I don't see how you can make them work together!"

8 "I have only four feet," Sonny said. "How many do you have, Pokey?"

9 "I have just one foot. It's my whole bottom side," Pokey said.

10 I started off down the path. When I looked back, I saw Sonny. He was down on his stomach, trying to move along on one "foot" just like Pokey.

162

Knowing the Words

Words that mean the same or nearly the same are **synonyms.** Circle two synonyms in each sentence below.

1. I laughed and Sonny chuckled.
2. My path is my road to the field.

Working with Words

Fill in each blank with the right pair of letters to make a word.

sh   ch

1. Foxes _____ased Uncle Bunny.
2. Sarah Jean hid under a bu_____.

Write these words. Draw a line to show the two syllables in each word.

3. ladder _____

4. corner _____

Add the word part **un-** to these words to finish the sentences below. One is done for you.

friendly   fair   lock   true

The game was *unfair*_____.

5. The new girl is _____.

6. Please _____ the door.

7. The last story is _____.

Reading and Thinking

1. Where did Sonny find Pokey's shell? _____

2. Number the sentences to show what happened first, second, third, and last.

____ Pokey appeared.

____ Sonny crawled like Pokey, on one foot.

____ Uncle Bunny stumbled.

____ Uncle Bunny tapped on Pokey's shell.

Write **T** if the sentence is true.
Write **F** if it is not true.

3. ____ Sonny was surprised that Pokey had just one foot.

4. ____ Sonny didn't know that Pokey was in his shell.

5. ____ Pokey is a speedy animal.

Sam Saves the Day

Read the story to find out how Uncle Bunny's cane helped the baby robins.

1 "Uncle Bunny! Hurry, please!" Sam Sparrow called to me. "We have to save Rosie's babies."

2 "Bless my ears and whiskers!" I cried. "What's wrong? Aren't the babies in the nest?"

3 "A storm cracked the branch where Rosie Robin has her nest. The branch is about to break," Sam shouted. "The babies are all alone in the nest. We have to help!"

4 We soon reached Rosie's tree. I could see that the branch was going to break very soon. Sam wasn't strong enough to lift the nest, and my paws were not made for climbing trees. We had to find another way.

5 "Maybe you can hop up on those rocks, Uncle Bunny," Sam said. "Then you can reach out and get the nest." I got myself up on the rocks, but I still couldn't reach the nest.

6 "Try your cane, Uncle Bunny," Sam said. My cane was just long enough. I pulled the nest toward me. At last I could lift it off the branch. Sam flew with me as I climbed off the rocks. Then the branch broke.

7 "My babies!" Rosie cried as she came back from finding food. "Where are my babies?"

8 "Sam's quick thinking kept your family safe," I explained.

9 "Thank you both!" Rosie said. "What good friends you are!"

164

Knowing the Words

Write the words from the story that have these meanings.

1. broke _____
   (Par. 3)

2. move up _____
   (Par. 6)

Working with Words

Circle the right word. Write it in the blank.

1. Hold on to the _____ of the kite. (string   spring)

2. We planted a _____ in the yard. (tree   free)

3. Say the word *bake.* Listen to the vowel sound of the word. In each word below, circle the two letters that stand for that sound.

   afraid   stay   away   paint

The letter *g* can stand for the sound of *j* as in *cage* and *g* as in *girl.* Circle words that have *g* as in *girl.* Cross out words that have *g* as in *cage.*

   girl   cage

4. gift   village   wagon   bag

5. danger   grumpy   large   again

6. dog   strange   orange   game

Reading and Thinking

1. Why is the story called "Sam Saves the Day"? _____

   _____

   _____

Write **T** if the sentence is true.
Write **F** if it is not true.

2. ____ Uncle Bunny climbs trees.

3. ____ Sparrows aren't very strong.

4. What do you think Rosie Robin may do after feeding the babies?

   _____

   _____

Worms Don't Tell

Can you keep a secret? See if you can guess Sonny's secret.

1   Sonny is keeping some kind of secret. Tomorrow is my birthday. It could be a birthday secret!

2   This morning he was lying under a tree. He was holding his mouth shut with both front paws. "What is wrong with your mouth, Sonny?" I asked.

3   "I'm trying to keep a secret," he said. "I'm so excited. I have to tell someone soon."

4   "I'll keep the secret if you share it with me," I told him.

5   "Oh, I can't, Grandpa," Sonny said. "You are part of the secret!"

6   "Well, you can always trust an earthworm with a secret," I said.

7   "That is a wonderful idea!" Sonny cried. Sonny looked all over but couldn't find an earthworm. He looked by rocks and under trees and in the grass. He looked like he would pop!

8   Just then Rosie Robin flew by. "Can I help?" she asked Sonny. "I'm an expert at finding worms." Rosie pushed her bill deep into the ground. Soon she pulled out a worm.

9   "Thank you, Rosie," Sonny called. Then he sat down and whispered to the worm for a long time.

10   I was very curious. I suppose I'll know soon. Sonny said, "When the Forest Story Teller tells just one more story, all of us will know."

Knowing the Words

Write the words from the story that have these meanings.

1. someone good
at something _____
(Par. 8)

2. wanting
to know _____
(Par. 10)

Working with Words

Use these words to make compound words. Then use the compound words to finish each sentence below.

earth   birth   worm   day

1. Come to my _____ party.

2. A bird found an _____.

An 's at the end of a word may be used to show that something belongs to someone. Change these groups of words using 's.

3. the secret of Sonny

_____

4. the nest of the bird

_____

5. the branch of the tree

_____

Reading and Thinking

1. Check the answer that tells what the story is mostly about.

____ keeping a secret

____ a worm

____ trouble with Sonny's mouth

2. What did Rosie Robin do to find an earthworm for Sonny?

_____

3. Check the sentence that tells why Sonny was holding his mouth.

____ His tooth hurt.

____ It was full of carrots.

____ He was keeping a secret.

4. Why couldn't Sonny share his

secret with Uncle Bunny? _____

_____

5. Check the sentence that tells why the worm can keep the secret.

____ Worms live in the ground.

____ Worms have no legs.

____ Worms cannot talk.

6. What do you think Sonny's secret

is? _____

A Well-Kept Secret

How do you know that Uncle Bunny has lots of friends in the forest?

1   "A rabbit's birthday should start with a carrot," I thought. I hopped toward the best carrot patch. I stopped when I saw something strange. Mrs. Buzz was showing Betsy Bear the tree where she keeps her honey. Most times they don't get along at all.

2   Farther along I stopped once more. I saw Red Squirrel. He was digging nuts for Barnie Raccoon.

3   At last I came to the carrot patch. Carol Anne and Sarah Jean had their cheeks stuffed with carrots. "These are for Sonny's secret. Don't chew them!" Carol Anne said.

4   By that time I was very hungry. I ate my fill of carrots. The sun was so warm I stretched out for a nap. Spotty Whitetail came to wake me. "Sonny needs you to come right now!" Spotty shouted.

5   When I reached the woods, I heard Sonny. "Over here, Grandpa," he called. I leaped over a bush and saw Sonny. He was carrying the biggest carrot cake I ever saw.

6   Voices from all over the forest cheered, "Happy birthday, Uncle Bunny!" One by one, my friends popped out of their hiding places.

7   "Bless my ears and whiskers!" I cried with surprise. "You are the best friends a rabbit could have!"

Reading and Thinking

1. Number the sentences to show what happened first, second, third, and last.

_____ Uncle Bunny's friends cheered, "Happy birthday!"

_____ Uncle Bunny saw some strange things happening.

_____ Uncle Bunny took a nap.

_____ Uncle Bunny decided to eat carrots for breakfast.

2. Write three things that were in Uncle Bunny's birthday cake.

_____

Working with Words

Rewrite these words to mean more than one. Remember to change the *y* to *i* before adding **-es.**

1. country _____

2. city _____

3. family _____

4. Say the word *keep*. Listen to the vowel sound in the word. In each word below, circle the two letters that stand for that sound.

feet   each   seed   deep

The spelling of some base words is changed before an ending is added. Words such as *happy* must have the *y* changed to *i* before adding an ending. Endings are word parts like **-er, -est,** and **-ed.** Change the *y* to *i* and add the endings to these words. One is done for you.

carry + ed _carried_____

5. heavy + est _____

6. hurry + ed _____

7. merry + er _____

8. hungry + est _____

169

Knowing the Words

Write the story words that have these meanings.

1. good or great

_____wonderful_____
(Par. 2)

2. place to keep coats

_____closet_____
(Par. 5)

3. went that way

_____headed_____
(Par. 5)

Reading and Thinking

1. This story is mostly about

___ Marta's chair.

_✓_ Marta's surprise.

___ Marta's breakfast.

Words such as *he, she,* and *it* take the place of other words. Read these sentences. Then fill in the blanks.

Marta shouted as she ran.

She stands for _Marta_.

2. Her mom laughed as she talked.

She stands for _her mom_.

3. My dad talked as he worked.

He stands for _my dad_.

3

Reading and Thinking

Put each word in the right blank.

nose   hair   leash

1. She wiggled her ____nose____

2. My dog has a new ____leash____

3. Does Nicky have short ____hair____

Circle the right answer.

4. What will Marta do next?

go to the library

(take Nicky home)

feed the birds

5. What helped Aunt Rosa train Nicky?

____a book____

Working with Words

Circle the best word for each sentence. Then write it in the blank.

1. Nicky ____ran____ to Mar

can (ran) pan

2. Marta walked her ____dog____

(dog) does did

3. Nicky wiggled her ____ear____

eat each (ear)

Knowing the Words

Write the story words that have these meanings.

1. walked fast

_____trotted_____
(Par. 1)

2. rope used to hold an animal

_____leash_____
(Par. 2)

3. ran after

_____chased_____
(Par. 2)

Reading and Thinking

1. What is the name of Lee's dog?

_____Bigfoot_____

Why do you think he is named that?

_____He has big feet._____

_____

2. What happened first in the story? Put **1** by it. What happened next? Put **2** by it. Put **3** by the thing that happened last.

_3_ Marta called to Christy and Joe.

_2_ Marta saw Lee and her dog.

_1_ Marta took Nicky to the park.

Reading and Thinking

1. What will Nicky's collar have on it?

____a brown tag with Marta's____

____name and phone number on it____

2. Why did Marta buy two dishes?

____one for food and one for water____

_____

3. Why did Marta pick a blue collar and blue dishes? ____She likes blue____

____best.____

Working with Words

Circle the best word for each sentence. Then write it in the blank.

1. The birds will ____fly____ aw

try bright (fly)

2. His hair is ____black____

break (black) drink

3. I am ____glad____ you are he

flew (glad) blue

4. Who will win the ____prize____

(prize) place grass

7

ite the story words that have
se meanings.

someone you like a lot

__friend__
(Par. 1)

someone who can carry things

__carrier__
(Par. 4)

cle the three words in each line
t belong together.

(house)　book　(park)　(store)
(bark)　fly　(wiggle)　(jump)
soup　(lunch)　(dinner)　(breakfast)
ball　(friend)　(neighbor)　(aunt)

---

1. This story is mostly about
   ✓ Nicky and the mail.
   ___ a bone for Nicky.
   ___ Mom's surprise.

2. Why does Nicky bark so much?

   She thinks the mail carrier is

   not a friend.

   _____

3. Can you think of a way to make Nicky stop barking?

   (Answers will vary.)

   _____

   _____

Some of these sentences are about **real** things, things that could happen. Write **R** by them. The other sentences are about things that could not happen, **make-believe** things. Write **M** by them.

1. _R_ A dog can run and play.
2. _M_ A house can talk.
3. _R_ A dog likes bones.
4. _M_ A dog likes to read.
5. Why does Mrs. Smith like her

   job? She likes to walk

   and talk to everyone.

   _____

Write each set of words in A-B-C order.

1. mail　bark　know

   ___bark___

   ___know___

   ___mail___

2. work　ears　please

   ___ears___

   ___please___

   ___work___

3. friend　carrier　drink

   ___carrier___

   ___drink___

   ___friend___

---

t each word in the right blank.

started　petted　burned

He ___started___ to go away.

The wood ___burned___ well.

We ___petted___ the cat.

ite **R** by the sentences that are
out **real** things. Write **M** by the
ntences about **make-believe**
ngs.

_M_ Dogs can bake bread.

_R_ People can bake bread.

_R_ People bake bread in an oven.

_M_ An oven keeps food cool.

A **base** word is a word without an ending. The words in each row have the same **base** word. Circle the ending of each one. Then write the **base** word in the blank.

1. call(ing)　　2. burn(ing)
   call(ed)　　　 burn(ed)
   cal(s)　　　　 burn(s)

   ___call___　　___burn___

Circle the best word for each sentence. Then write it in the blank.

3. We'll eat ___when___ he comes.
   then　(when)　check

4. Please finish ___those___ apples.
   chase　(those)　shoes

---

1. Marta and Lee went to the

   creek because __it was cool__

   __there__ .

2. Why couldn't Nicky find any

   fish after she jumped in? They

   hid from her.

3. Write **1, 2,** and **3** by these sentences to show what happened first, next, and last.

   _3_ Nicky jumped into the water.

   _1_ Lee said, "Stop for a while!"

   _2_ Nicky sniffed the water.

Write each set of words in A-B-C order.

1. tired　idea　creek

   ___creek___

   ___idea___

   ___tired___

2. quiet　sniffed　fish

   ___fish___

   ___quiet___

   ___sniffed___

3. splash　cool　jumped

   ___cool___

   ___jumped___

   ___splash___

Write the story words that have these meanings.

1. run after

   <u>chase</u>
   (Par. 3)

2. moved the head up and down

   <u>nodded</u>
   (Par. 6)

3. people who live near you

   <u>neighbors</u>
   (Par. 7)

Put a check by the meaning that fits the underlined word in each sentence.

4. Is it <u>hard</u> to make new friends?
   ___ something not soft
   _✓_ something not easy to do

5. I will <u>watch</u> Nicky play.
   ___ thing that tells time
   _✓_ look at

1. What kind of dog is Flash?

   <u>collie</u>

2. This story is mostly about
   ___ Marta playing with Nicky.
   _✓_ a new neighbor.
   ___ Nicky's ball.

3. How will Nicky and Marta help Mike with his dog? <u>(Answers will vary.)</u>

   _____

4. Flash can't do any tricks because <u>he is not trained</u>

   _____

1. This story is mostly about
   ___ Nicky playing.
   _✓_ Nicky finding a kitten.
   ___ Nicky holding a kitten.

2. The four dogs were barking because <u>a little cat was on top of the car</u>

3. What makes you think that Nicky likes kittens? <u>(Answers will vary.)</u>

   _____

Circle the best word for each sentence. Then write it in the blank.

1. This <u>cat</u> likes r
   (cat)   call   cut

2. I will <u>get</u> a dri
   gave   got   (get)

Write -**ing** or -**ed** in each blank.

3. I talk <u>ed</u> with her yesterday.

4. She want <u>ed</u> to work.

5. Now she is help <u>ing</u> us.

Circle the right word for each sentence. Then write it in the blank.

6. Mike is my best <u>friend</u>
   ground   proud   (friend)

7. I need a <u>drink</u> of wat
   trick   (drink)   break

Look at each picture and circle the sentence that goes with it.

1. (Nicky is playing outside.)

   Nicky is playing in the house.

2. Nicky sleeps on Marta's bed.

   (Nicky sleeps in her basket.)

3. Who fixed dinner? <u>Dad</u>

4. How did Nicky carry the kitten?

   <u>in her mouth</u>

5. Why did Marta stay outside?

   <u>(Answers will vary.)</u>

Circle the best word for each sentence. Then write it in the blank.

1. Nicky's collar has a <u>tag</u>.
   (tag)   than   tail

2. Nicky can be a <u>quiet</u> dog.
   get   (quiet)   paint

3. The little kitten was <u>wet</u>.
   pet   met   (wet)

Write these sentences. Use one of the shorter words from the box to stand for the words that are underlined.

| we'll isn't can't didn't I'm |

4. <u>We will</u> be there.

   <u>We'll be there.</u>

5. He <u>did not</u> go.

   <u>He didn't go.</u>

6. The kitten <u>is not</u> hurt.

   <u>The kitten isn't hurt.</u>

7. <u>I am</u> hungry.

   <u>I'm hungry.</u>

8. Flash <u>cannot</u> do tricks.

   <u>Flash can't do tricks.</u>

1. This story is mostly about
   ___ warming the milk.
   ___ talking about dogs.
   _✓_ the kitten's new home.

Fill in the blanks.

2. Mom said, "Good idea," as she warmed the milk.

   She stands for <u>Mom</u>

3. Mom found a box and lined it with a blanket.

   It stands for <u>box</u>

Circle the best word for each sentence. Then write it in the blank.

1. The milk is too <u>hot</u>
   hit   (hot)   hat

2. The kitten's eyes are <u>big</u>
   (big)   bag   buy

3. Marta's mom made a <u>bed</u>
   back   (bed)   bird

4. They have a <u>new</u> pe
   now   not   (new)

Read these words and look at the pictures.

Marta's mom   her mom's har

You can see that you add 's wher you want to show that the hand belongs to Mom. Now write thes names the same way.

5. Marta <u>Marta's</u> har

6. Mike <u>Mike's</u> har

Knowing the Words

Write the story words that have these meanings.

someone who keeps you well

doctor
(Par. 3)

to be well

healthy
(Par. 3)

to look over with care

check
(Par. 4)

Circle the three words in each line that belong together.

(arms) flowers (feet) (hands)
(eyes) (ears) doctor (mouth)
hair (brown) (white) (black)

Reading and Thinking

1. This story is mostly about
   ___ pets who are not well.
   ___ a mean doctor.
   ✓ keeping pets healthy.

2. What four things did the doctor check on Nicky and Inky?

   coats

   eyes

   ears

   mouths

3. What do you think Marta can do to keep her pets healthy?

   (Answers will vary.)

   _____

   _____

27

Reading and Thinking

Put each word in the right blank.

puppy   learn   door

1. Please open the ___door___.

2. Children ___learn___ at school.

3. My ___puppy___ has black eyes.

4. Write **1, 2,** and **3** by these sentences to show what happened first, next, and last.

   _3_ Marta was glad to see her friends.

   _2_ Nicky barked and ran to the door.

   _1_ There was a knock on the door.

29

Working with Words

Circle the best word for each sentence. Then write it in the blank.

1. Can you read this ___book___?
   cook   look   (book)

2. Marta ___met___ Allen today.
   mail   (met)   mean

3. Nicky pounded her ___tail___ on the floor.
   (tail)   fill   well

The missing word in each sentence sounds like *right*. Change the *r* in *right* to *f, l,* or *n*. Write the new words. The first one is done.

4. *fight*   light   night

Use the words you made in sentences.

5. Please turn off the ___light___.

6. We will not ___fight___ over the toys.

7. It rained last ___night___.

Knowing the Words

Write the story words that have these meanings.

not hard

easy
(Par. 1)

what you call someone

name
(Par. 1)

Circle the three words in each line that belong together.

(walk) look (trot) (run)
(head) (tail) trick (feet)
(good) mean (great) (wonderful)

Reading and Thinking

1. This story is mostly about
   ___ how to pet your dog.
   ✓ a meeting at Marta's.
   ___ Mike's dog.

2. What did Marta say a dog must know first?

   its name

3. Tell one important lesson that Lee learned. ___You have___
   ___to show a dog you're happy___
   ___it did something right.___

4. Why do you think a dog learns faster if you say "good dog"?

   (Answers will vary.)

   _____

   _____

Reading and Thinking

1. This story is mostly about
   ✓ brushing dogs.
   ___ brushing Marta's hair.
   ___ Marta's dad.

2. Marta's dad said Nicky looked like a ___string mop___

3. Why should you talk quietly and pet your dog when you brush it?

   (Answers will vary.)

   _____

   _____

Working with Words

Circle the best word for each sentence. Then write it in the blank.

1. Birds like to ___use___ hair in their nests.
   us   up   (use)

2. I can ___bake___ bread.
   back   (bake)   book

3. I ___like___ to brush my dog.
   little   (like)   let

Read these words and look at the pictures.

cat   cats

You can see that you add *s* to show that you mean more than one cat. Write these words so that they mean more than one.

4. dog ___dogs___

5. bird ___birds___

6. ear ___ears___

Knowing the Words: Word meaning from context (1-2); Classification (3-5). **Reading and Thinking:** Main idea (1); Facts and details (2-3); Drawing conclusions (4).

31

33

Put each word in the right blank.

special   bath   letter

1. Why is today so ___special___?

2. Nicky likes her ___bath___.

3. Marta wrote a ___letter___.

4. Who trained Nicky to sit?

   _____Aunt Rosa_____

5. What is going to happen soon?

   _____a dog show_____

6. This letter is mostly about

   ___ Marta and her friends.

   ___ the special trick.

   _✓_ Nicky.

Write each set of words in A-B-C order.

1. trained   bath   special

   _____bath_____

   _____special_____

   _____trained_____

2. care   splash   trick

   _____care_____

   _____splash_____

   _____trick_____

3. pet   basket   sleeps

   _____basket_____

   _____pet_____

   _____sleeps_____

Put each word in the right blank.

hide   clean   delighted

1. My hands are ___clean___.

2. I am ___delighted___ to see you.

3. Will Nicky ___hide___ this bone from me?

4. Why do you think that Marta's grandmother and grandfather like dogs? _____

   (Answers will vary.)

Circle the best word for each sentence. Then write it in the blank.

1. Nicky has a cold ___nose___
   (nose)   not   now

2. We will ___take___ a wal
   talk   (take)   tail

The missing word in each sentence sounds like *make*. Change the *m* in *make* to *b, t,* or *w*. Write the new words.

3. ___bake___   ___take___   ___wake___

Use the words you made in sentences.

4. May we ___take___ a wa

5. I like to ___bake___ brea

6. Did Nicky ___wake___ yo

You know that *Mom's hand* mean "the hand of Mom." Add *'s* wher you write these names to show what belongs to each.

7. Dad   ___Dad's___ co

8. Mike   ___Mike's___ bo

9. Nicky   ___Nicky's___ tee

Write the story words that have these meanings.

1. work you do

   _____job_____
   (Par. 1)

2. made a low sound

   _____growled_____
   (Par. 5)

Put a check by the meaning that fits the underlined word in each sentence.

3. The blanket will <u>brush</u> Nicky's nose.

   ___ thing used to fix hair

   _✓_ move over softly

4. Will Dad <u>play</u> with Nicky?

   _✓_ have fun

   ___ a show

1. Who cleaned up after breakfast? _____Marta_____

2. How did Inky help? ___He___ ___drank the milk.___

Write **R** by the sentences that are **real** things. Write **M** by the sentences that are about **make-believe** things.

3. _R_ People can make beds.

4. _M_ Dogs can make beds.

5. _M_ Cats can weed flowers.

6. _R_ People can weed flowers.

Put each word in the right blank.

streams   hose   dry

1. We use a ___hose___ to water our flowers.

2. ___Streams___ of water ran down the window.

3. Is the paint ___dry___?

Write **R** by the sentences that are about **real** things. Write **M** by the sentences about **make-believe** things.

4. _M_ A yard can walk.

5. _R_ A dog can walk.

6. _R_ Birds can fly.

7. _M_ Dogs can fly.

Circle the best word for each sentence. Then write it in the blank.

1. She likes to ___pick___ flowers.
   pet   pan   (pick)

2. Sit ___back___ and rea
   (back)   bake   best

3. I like ___that___ bo
   think   thank   (that)

Fill in the missing vowel (*i, o,* or *u*) so the sentence makes sense.

4. Write on the l_i_ne.

5. Please give Nicky a b_o_ne

6. May Nicky _u_se this pan?

Fill in each blank with **str** or **spr** the sentence makes sense.

7. Here is a ball of ___str___ing.

8. I will ___spr___ay the grass.

9. Don't walk in the ___str___eet.

Reading and Thinking

each word in the right blank.

cost   spend   bicycle

I have a new ___bicycle___.

I will ___spend___ my own money.

Does this ball ___cost___ much?

in the blanks.

Flash's ball fell so Nicky carried it.

It stands for ___ball___.

Marta and Nicky were happy because they were helping.

They stands for ___Marta___ and ___Nicky___.

Nicky was carrying the ball as she ran.

She stands for ___Nicky___

Working with Words

Circle the best word for each sentence. Then write it in the blank.

1. Did Marta ___train___ Nicky?
    day   tail   (train)

2. Can you ___hear___ Nicky bark?
    heel   (hear)   head

3. Put on your warm ___coat___.
    (coat)   cook   clean

Change each underlined word to two words. Write them on the line.

4. Flash <u>didn't</u> have a ball.

    ___did not___

5. This <u>isn't</u> my bicycle.

    ___is not___

Circle the right letters for each sentence. Then write them in the blank.

6. I st___ar___ted to sit up.
    er   (ar)   ir

7. This book is too sh___or___t.
    (or)   er   at

8. Did the salesp___er___son help?
    or   (er)   ar

43

Knowing the Words

Write the story words that have these meanings.

1. moved on the air

    ___floated___
    (Par. 2)

2. trees with leaves that stay green

    ___evergreens___
    (Par. 2)

3. came to the ground

    ___landed___
    (Par. 2)

Put a check by the meaning that fits the underlined word in the sentence.

4. Did Marta know how to throw the airplane <u>right</u>?

    ___ not on the left

    ✓ not the wrong way

Reading and Thinking

Put each word in the right blank.

owned   proud   evergreens

1. I am ___proud___ of my dog.

2. We planted ___evergreens___ in our yard.

3. Mike ___owned___ a new toy.

4. Write **1, 2,** and **3** by these sentences to show what happened first, next, and last.

    __2__ Nicky shook Mike's toy.

    __1__ Mike got an airplane.

    __3__ Marta said that she would buy another airplane.

5. Why does Marta want to buy Mike a new airplane?

    ___(Answers will vary.)___

45

Reading and Thinking

When you are weeding, why do you have to know the flowers from the weeds?

    ___(Answers will vary.)___

Why did Nicky try to jump on the broom? ___She wanted to play.___

What did Marta do to make Nicky understand she was not playing a game? ___She shouted and shook the broom.___

Working with Words

Read each sentence and circle the word that is made of two shorter words. Write the two words on the lines.

1. You can sweep the (sidewalk).

    ___side___   ___walk___

2. Nicky did not (understand).

    ___under___   ___stand___

3. Will (someone) please help?

    ___some___   ___one___

Circle the best word for each sentence. Then write it in the blank.

4. Please ___show___ us a trick.
    who   (show)   those

5. Where are your ___shoes___?
    this   who's   (shoes)

6. Nicky will ___chase___ me.
    shook   (chase)   shout

47

Reading and Thinking

Look at each picture and circle the sentence that goes with it.

1. (Nicky likes the water.)

    Nicky does not like the water.

2. A mother can work.

    (A mother can read.)

3. (He loves Bigfoot.)

    He doesn't like Bigfoot.

4. Where are the children working with Bigfoot?

    ___at Lee's house___

    How do you know? ___(Answers will vary.)___

Working with Words

Write these sentences. Use one shorter word for the two words that are underlined.

1. She <u>does not</u> know my name.

    ___She doesn't know my name.___

2. Bigfoot <u>will not</u> sit.

    ___Bigfoot won't sit.___

3. <u>It is</u> a beautiful day.

    ___It's a beautiful day.___

4. <u>I am</u> glad today.

    ___I'm glad today.___

Write these words so that they mean more than one. One is done for you.

    house   *houses*

5. mother   ___mothers___

6. dog   ___dogs___

7. boy   ___boys___

49

Knowing the Words

Write the story words that have these meanings.

1. thing that shows pictures

   <u>television</u>
   <small>(Par. 1)</small>

2. ideas or ways of doing

   something <u>plans</u>
   <small>(Par. 1)</small>

3. room used for cooking

   <u>kitchen</u>
   <small>(Par. 1)</small>

Put a check by the meaning that fits the underlined word in each sentence.

4. Nicky <u>can</u> shut the door.

   _____ a thing to hold food

   _✓_ knows how to

5. I must <u>check</u> for the newspaper.

   _____ make a line

   _✓_ look with care

Reading and Thinking

1. Why do you think Marta's dad didn't open the door himself?

   <u>(Answers will vary.)</u>

   _____

2. Do you think Nicky will shut the door again? _____

   Why or why not? _____

   <u>(Answers will vary.)</u>

   _____

3. Write **1, 2,** and **3** by these sentences to show what happened first, next, and last.

   _2_ Marta's dad looked for the newspaper.

   _1_ Marta's dad watched television.

   _3_ Marta saw Nicky's new trick.

51

Reading and Thinking

1. Why did Nicky wake up?

   <u>Inky jumped on her.</u>

   _____

Put each word in the right blank.

   wonderful   wake   piece

2. Warm bread smells

   <u>wonderful</u>.

3. Please give me a <u>piece</u> of bread.

4. Will you <u>wake</u> me?

Working with Words

The missing word in each sentence sounds like *stop*. Change the *st* in *stop* to *t, m,* or *p.* Write the new words and put them in the right sentences.

1. <u>top</u>   <u>mop</u>   <u>pop</u>

2. Some popcorn didn't <u>pop</u>

3. I hit the <u>top</u> of my hea

4. Clean the floor with a <u>mop</u>

Circle the right letters for each sentence. Then write them in the blank.

5. They walked in the p_<u>ar</u>_k

   er   ir   (ar)

6. What happened f_<u>ir</u>_st?

   ar   or   (ir)

Add *'s* to these words to show what belongs to each one.

7. dog   the <u>dog's</u> col

8. cat   the <u>cat's</u> hea

9. bird   the <u>bird's</u> nes

10. kitten   the <u>kitten's</u> bal

Knowing the Words

Write the story words that have these meanings.

1. near

   <u>close</u>
   <small>(Par. 4)</small>

2. so glad

   <u>delighted</u>
   <small>(Par. 5)</small>

Circle the three words in each line that belong together.

3. (paws) (tail) soft (head)

4. (glad)(delighted)(pleased) sad

5. paint (grass) (park) (yard)

Reading and Thinking

1. This story is mostly about

   _____ a fast car.

   _____ Mike's bicycle.

   _✓_ Marta helping Flash.

2. Why was Flash walking in the street by himself? <u>Mike wasn't</u>

   <u>there to tell him "no."</u>

3. How had the dog lessons helped Flash? <u>He came when</u>

   <u>Marta called him.</u>

4. Write **1, 2,** and **3** to show what happened first, next, and last.

   _3_ Flash ran to Marta.

   _2_ Marta called to Flash.

   _1_ Marta played in her yard.

Reading and Thinking

1. What did Marta think was

   better than a bath? <u>using the</u>

   <u>hose to get clean</u>

2. Why did Marta's dad help her

   call Mike? <u>Marta was</u>

   <u>too muddy to go inside.</u>

Put each word in the right blank.

   belongs   mud   swimsuit

3. Flash has <u>mud</u> on him.

4. This book <u>belongs</u> to Allen.

5. My <u>swimsuit</u> is too big.

Working with Words

Fill in the missing vowel (a, i, or o) so each sentence makes sense.

1. You did a f_<u>i</u>_ne job.

2. Wash off with the h_<u>o</u>_se.

3. We will m_<u>a</u>_ke the bed.

Use the underlined words to make a new word to finish each sentence.

4. A <u>suit</u> that you wear when you

   <u>swim</u> is called a <u>swimsuit</u>

5. A <u>yard</u> that is in <u>back</u> of a

   house is called a <u>backyard</u>

Circle the best word for each sentence. Then write it in the blank.

6. Do not <u>shout</u> at me

   show   (shout)   chair

7. Our house is <u>clean</u>

   boat   (clean)   stay

55

Reading and Thinking

[P]ut each word in the right blank.

quiet   lapping   television

The cat is ___lapping___ up the milk.

What ___television___ show do you like best?

We were ___quiet___ in the library.

This story is mostly about

___✓___ Inky's trick.

_____ Mom and Dad needing quiet.

_____ Nicky wants to play.

Working with Words

To make a word mean more than one, add -es if the word ends in s, ss, ch, sh, or x. Write these words so that they mean more than one.

1. lunch   ___lunches___

2. dish   ___dishes___

3. box   ___boxes___

Fill in the missing letter so the sentence makes sense.

4. I like to h_e_lp my dad.

5. Nicky j_u_mped into the water.

6. Marta p_i_cked up the ball.

Fill in the missing letters so each sentence makes sense.

ar   or   ur

7. Did Nicky h_ur_t her paw?

8. Can we play in your y_ar_d?

59

Knowing the Words

Write the story words that have these meanings.

1. part of a house ___basement___
(Par. 1)

2. close ___near___
(Par. 1)

3. to wash off ___clean___
(Par. 5)

4. top part of a house ___upstairs___
(Par. 5)

5. place in back of a house ___backyard___
(Par. 6)

Circle the three words in each line that belong together.

6. (upstairs) idea (house) (kitchen)

7. (chair) (table) mail (picture)

8. box (brush) (broom) (mop)

9. (ran) sat (raced) (chased)

Reading and Thinking

1. If you paint in dusty air, how will the paint look? ___dusty___

___(Answers will vary.)___

2. How did Marta's mom and dad's work look when it was done?

___good___

Look at each picture and circle the sentence that goes with it.

3. (Dad paints with a brush.)

Dad is brushing Nicky.

4. (Joe helps at home.)

Joe is not helping.

61

Reading and Thinking

Where did Mom and Dad go after dinner? ___the backyard___

Marta wanted to do the dishes because ___she wanted___

___everyone to help___

Write 1, 2, and 3 to show what happened first, next, and last.

_2_ Marta washed the dinner dishes.

_3_ Marta washed the pets' dishes.

_1_ Marta had dinner.

Working with Words

In each row, circle the two letters in each word that make the same sound you hear in the underlined word.

toy   point   boy   noise

1. show   kn(ow)   (ow)n   thr(ow)

2. see   tr(ee)   f(ee)t   pl(ea)se

3. found   d(ow)n   ar(ou)nd   br(ow)n

4. mean   n(ee)d   n(ea)r   r(ea)d

Circle the best word for each sentence. Then write it in the blank.

5. Do you like this ___game___?
   same   (game)   name

6. Mike found ___his___ money.
   hit   him   (his)

7. This is my ___best___ hat.
   (best)   nest   last

8. Marta hit the ___ball___.
   (ball)   call   tell

Circle each c that stands for the sound of s in these words.

9. on(c)e   12. pie(c)e

10. doctor   13. because

11. fen(c)e   14. come

63

Knowing the Words

Write the story words that have these meanings.

1. push on

___lean___
(Par. 3)

2. what a dog has around its neck ___collar___
(Par. 7)

3. made a noise in the nose ___snorted___
(Par. 7)

Circle the three words in each line that belong together.

4. mail   (library)   (store)   (park)

5. (heel)   (sit)   (stay)   found

6. (collar)   (leash)   (tag)   bird

7. (move)   (walk)   (run)   stay

Reading and Thinking

Look at each picture and circle the sentence that goes with it.

1. Dogs and cats do not like each other.

(The dog and cat are friends.)

2. (Marta likes to read books.)

Marta never reads books.

3. Why did Bigfoot snort?

___He didn't like it when he___

___fell over.___

4. Why do you think Mr. Barker knows a lot about dogs?

___(Answers will vary.)___

_____

65

Reading and Thinking

1. This story is mostly about
   ____ the prize ribbons.
   ____ going to the library.
   _✓_ the dog show.

2. What five things do the children need for their dog show?

   _____ signs _____

   _____ rope _____

   _____ number signs _____

   _____ ribbons _____

   _____ prizes _____

3. Who will make the copies?

   _____ Lee _____

Working with Words

Circle the right letters for each sentence. Then write them in the blank.

1. Do you w__or__k hard?
   ar (or) ir

2. It is your t__ur__n to play.
   ar   or (ur)

3. The dog sn__or__ts loudly.
   er (or) ar

Circle the best word for each sentence. Then write it in the blank.

4. Can you make your __bed__?
   bag (bed) big

5. Mike wrote a __letter__.
   listen last (letter)

6. We filled the __pan__ with milk.
   (pan) pet pop

Use the underlined words to make a new word to finish each sentence.

7. Corn that can pop when you cook it is __popcorn__.

8. A walk that is by the side of the street is a __sidewalk__.

67

Reading and Thinking

1. Why did Marta ask if Dad had to go away the day of the show?

   __She thought he might not be__

   __able to come to the show.__

   _____

Fill in the blanks.

2. Mom and Dad talked as they painted.
   They stands for

   __Mom and Dad__

3. Marta's dad answered, and he said, "No, Marta."

   He stands for __Marta's dad__.

Working with Words

The missing word in each sentence sounds like *new*. Change the *n* in *new* to *bl*, *fl*, and *thr*. Write the new words, and pu them in the right sentences.

1. __blew__ __flew__ __threw__

2. The wind __blew__ har

3. I __threw__ my dog a ba

4. The bird __flew__ awa

Circle the best word for each sentence. Then write it in the blan

5. Marta will __brush__ Nick
   grass (brush) growl

6. Will Dad __try__ to be here
   dry play (try)

The ending **-er** means "more" and the ending **-est** means "most." Add the endings **-er** and **-est** to these base words.

	-er	**-est**
clean	*cleaner*	*clean*
7. kind	kinder	kindest
8. fast	faster	fastest

6

Knowing the Words

Write the story words that have these meanings.

1. to lean over

   _____ bend _____
   (Par. 1)

2. moved hand up and down

   _____ waved _____
   (Par. 2)

3. thinking of others

   _____ kind _____
   (Par. 4)

Put a check by the meaning that fits the underlined word in each sentence.

4. Why did Mom say that?
   _✓_ a word that asks something
   ____ a word of surprise

5. Why, Marta, that's beautiful!
   ____ a word that asks something
   _✓_ a word of surprise

Reading and Thinking

Put each word in the right blank.
   waved   bend   tired

1. Those jobs make me __tired__.

2. I __waved__ to my friend.

3. The flowers will __bend__ in the wind.

4. How are Marta and Mrs. Peters helping each other?

   __Marta is holding the basket,__

   __and Mrs. Peters will make__

   __the ribbons. (Answers may__

   __vary.)__

Reading and Thinking

Look at each picture and circle the sentence that goes with it.

1. Nicky is asleep in her basket.

   (Nicky has a bone.)

2. Inky is jumping.

   (Inky is drinking milk.)

3. (Mike cuts the grass.)

   Mike weeds the flowers.

Put each word in the right blank.
   spray   shiny   enter

4. Marta has __shiny__ new shoes.

5. We __spray__ the flowers.

6. Please knock and __enter__.

71

Working with Words

Write these words so that they mean more than one.

1. sign __signs__

2. idea __ideas__

3. can __cans__

Circle the best word for each sentence. Then write it in the blank.

4. Dad __cooked__ breakfast
   cooking (cooked)

5. Mom is __working__ outside
   works (working)

6. Grandfather __wants__ to help
   (wants) wanting

7. We can plant a __garden__
   good (garden) judge

8. Do you live in the __city__
   coat (city) cut

9. Please __let__ me go
   (let) lot last

10. She has a funny __hat__
    (hat) hit hot

73

Reading and Thinking

Why would the pet shop be a good place for a dog show sign?

People who have or like

dogs come to that shop.

___

To tell where the prizes came from at the show, Mike will say, "Today's prizes are from

Mr. Barker's pet store

___."

Do you think Mr. Barker will be a good judge for the show? ___

Why do you think so? _____

(Answers will vary.)

___

Working with Words

Circle the best word for each sentence. Then write it in the blank.

1. What is __better__ than a bath?
basket   basement   (better)

2. Please __check__ your work.
(check)   collar   closet

Write these sentences. Use one shorter word for the two words that are underlined.

3. I do not have a sign.

I don't have a sign.

4. That is great!

That's great!

5. We will be glad.

We'll be glad.

6. That is not a good place.

That isn't a good place.

75

Reading and Thinking

Put each word in the right blank.
entered   glitter   prizes

1. This __glitter__ will make the ribbon shiny.

2. Lee __entered__ her dog in the show.

3. We will give ribbons for __prizes__.

4. How did Mike and Marta get a can full of money? __People gave it to them to enter the dog show.__

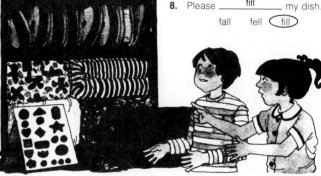

77

Working with Words

Sometimes the letter c stands for the sound s makes as in city. Circle each c that stands for the sound of s in these words.

1. (c)ircle   3. (c)ity
2. cat   4. car

Circle the best word for each sentence. Then write it in the blank.

5. I know __what__ you want.
(what)   shut   that

6. I'll be __there__ in a minute.
chair   (there)   where

7. The __wind__ blew hard.
will   well   (wind)

8. Please __fill__ my dish.
fall   fell   (fill)

Reading and Thinking

Put each word in the right blank.
permission   paste   nodded

Marta __nodded__ her head.

I have __permission__ to go.

__Paste__ will make the ribbon stick together.

Who called the people who run the park? __Mom__

How do you think Mike and Joe felt while they were helping with the ribbons? __(Answers will vary.)__

Learning to Study

Write each set of words in A-B-C order.

1. people   money   other

money

other

people

2. busy   paste   cost

busy

cost

paste

3. glitter   ribbon   city

city

glitter

ribbon

79

Reading and Thinking

1. Who made the number signs?

Marta and Mike

2. What do you think Nicky was sniffing on Grandmother's coat?

Aunt Rosa (Answers may vary.)

3. Write 1, 2, and 3 to show what happened first, next, and last.

__3__ Aunt Rosa said, "Nicky, sit!"

__2__ Grandfather talked to Marta.

__1__ Mom knocked on Marta's door.

Working with Words

In each sentence, circle the word that is made of two shorter words. Write the two words on the lines.

(Everyone) met at Lee's house.

Every   *one*

1. Do you ever play (football)?

foot   ball

2. (Grandmother) gave Marta a hug.

Grand   mother

Circle the best word for each sentence. Then write it in the blank.

3. They played with __their__ toys.
chair   (their)   where

4. I am __third__ in line.
while   short   (third)

In each row, circle the two letters in each word that stand for the vowel sound you hear in the underlined word.

5. day   p(ai)nt   tr(ai)n   st(ay)
6. each   gr(ee)n   m(ea)n   f(ee)t
7. know   c(oa)t   sh(ow)   (ow)n
8. proud   d(ow)n   ab(ou)t   n(ow)

81

Knowing the Words

Write the story words that have these meanings.

1. afraid

    _____nervous_____
    _(Par. 1)

2. a number of people together

    _____crowd_____
    _(Par. 1)

3. place for a dog show

    _____ring_____
    _(Par. 5)

Put a check by the meaning that fits the underlined word in each sentence.

4. Marta <u>saw</u> Lee standing there.

    ____ something that cuts wood

    ✓ used her eyes

5. Marta walked into the <u>ring</u>.

    ____ sound a telephone makes

    ✓ a circle where a show is

Reading and Thinking

Put each word in the right blank.

crowd   judge   nervous

1. The _____crowd_____ of people clapped.

2. Who will _____judge_____ the dog show?

3. She is _____nervous_____ about the show.

4. How did Nicky feel at the dog show? _____(Answers will vary.)_____

5. How do you think Nicky and Marta will do in the show?

    _____(Answers will vary.)_____

Reading and Thinking

1. Why couldn't Mr. Barker pick a winner? _____All of the dogs_____ _____in the ring were well trained._____

    _____

2. What makes you think that Marta did not know about the gold ribbon?

    _____She looked in surprise at_____ _____Mrs. Peters._____

3. Why did the crowd pick Nicky to win? _____(Answers will vary.)_____

    _____

Working with Words

Circle the best word for each sentence. Then write it in the blank.

1. I am still _____clapping_____ fo Nicky.

    clapped   (clapping)

2. Nicky _____jumped_____ over Marta

    (jumped)   jumping

Add 's to these words to show what belongs to each one. Write the new word.

3. judge   _____judge's_____ smile

4. Marta   _____Marta's_____ turn

5. Nicky   _____Nicky's_____ ribbo

Circle g when it stands for the sound of g in go.

6. (g)ood   8. judge
7. (g)arden   9. a(g)ain

83

8

Knowing the Words

Write the words from the story that have these meanings.

1. face hairs _____whiskers_____
    _(Par. 1)

2. did over and over _____practiced_____
    _(Par. 3)

3. did write _____wrote_____
    _(Par. 7)

Working with Words

Circle the right word to finish the sentence. Then write the word in the blank.

1. The team ran a good _____race_____.
    (face, case, (race))

2. Hit the ball with the _____bat_____.
    (bell, (bat), bed)

Reading and Thinking

1. Check the answer that tells what the story is mostly about.

    ____ how children learn

    ____ Uncle Bunny's big ears

    ✓ how Uncle Bunny learned to write

2. Look at the picture. Check the two sentences that tell about the picture.

    ✓ Uncle Bunny wears glasses.

    ____ Uncle Bunny drives a car.

    ✓ Uncle Bunny can write.

3. Uncle Bunny found a box under a

    _____window at the school_____

Some things are real and some are make-believe. Write **R** by real things. Write **M** by make-believe things.

4. _M_ Rabbits can write.

5. _R_ Children can learn.

6. _M_ Squirrels can talk.

Knowing the Words

Write the words from the story that have these meanings.

1. kind of plant _____clover_____
    _(Par. 1)

2. storm sound _____thunder_____
    _(Par. 1)

3. loud sounds _____noise_____
    _(Par. 3)

The words *come* and *go* have meanings so different that they are **opposite.** Make a line from each word in the first list to the word in the second list with the opposite meaning.

4. wet   noise
5. quiet   dry
6. stay ——————— leave

Working with Words

A word without any endings is a **base word.** The base word of *talking* is *talk*. Circle each base word below.

1. (listen)s   2. (push)ed   3. (eat)ing

Sometimes one word stands for two words. The word *didn't* stands for *did not*. Write a word from the story that can stand for each pair of words.

4. we will _____we'll_____
    _(Par. 4)

5. I am _____I'm_____
    _(Par. 5)

Reading and Thinking

1. Check the answer that tells what the story is mostly about.

    ____ Uncle Bunny having lunch

    ✓ where animals go during a storm

    ____ black clouds

2. Where were Mrs. Whitetail and Spotty when they heard thunder?

    _____under the trees_____

3. Check the sentence that tells why the deer moved to the open field.

    ____ They went there to eat.

    ____ Spotty tried to run away.

    ✓ A storm was coming.

4. Why do you think Spotty tried to run away? _____

    _____(Answers will vary.)_____

87

Knowing the Words

Write the words from the story that have these meanings.

a small place ___patch___
(Par. 1)

hair cut from sheep ___wool___
(Par. 4)

between cold and warm ___cool___
(Par. 7)

Circle the three words in each row that belong together.

(morning) year (night) (afternoon)
(coats) (hats) feet (shoes)
wet (cold) (warm) (hot)
(happy) (sad) (angry) old

Learning to Study

Number the words to show A-B-C order for each list.

1.
_3_ lamb
_1_ carrot
_2_ friend
_4_ wool

2.
_2_ cool
_1_ answered
_3_ patch
_4_ wrote

Reading and Thinking

1. Check the answer that tells what the story is mostly about.
   ___ keeping people warm
   ___ being cool in the summer
   _✓_ Sniffles giving his wool

2. What was Sniffles doing by the pond? ___looking at himself in the water___

3. Sniffles thought he looked funny because ___he didn't have his coat anymore___

Words such as *he*, *his*, *she*, and *her* take the place of other words. Read these sentences. Fill in the blanks.

4. Sniffles cried as he saw himself.
   He stands for ___Sniffles___

5. Uncle Bunny ate his carrots.
   His stands for ___Uncle Bunny___

Write **R** by the real things. Write **M** by the make-believe things.

6. _M_ Lambs wear gloves.

7. _R_ Coats are made from wool.

91

Knowing the Words

Write the words from the story that have these meanings.

1. one who takes something ___thief___
(Par. 1)

2. nut from oak tree ___acorn___
(Par. 3)

Check the meaning that fits the underlined word in each sentence.

3. We clean up leaves in the <u>fall.</u>
   _✓_ part of year before winter
   ___ to drop suddenly

4. I <u>wave</u> as I leave for school.
   _✓_ make a good-bye sign
   ___ rolling water

Working with Words

Write **S** beside each word that stands for one of something. Write **P** by each word that stands for more than one.

1. _S_ noise   2. _P_ acorns

Circle the right word to finish each sentence. Then write the word in the blank.

3. The cold wind ___blew___ in our faces. (threw, flew, (blew))

4. The cars hit with a loud ___crash___. (splash, (crash) flash)

Reading and Thinking

1. Red Squirrel planted an acorn in what part of the year? ___fall___

Write **T** if the sentence is true.
Write **F** if it is not true.

2. _T_ Oak trees grow from acorns.

3. _T_ The story happens in winter.

4. Red could not find his acorn because ___he didn't remember where he put it___

5. What do you think Red did after he ran up the tree? ___
   ___(Answers will vary.)___

6. How did Red Squirrel feel when he thought someone took his nut?
   ___angry___

93

Knowing the Words

Write the words from the story that have these meanings.

. black and
white animal ___skunk___
(Par. 1)

. small animals such
as bees and ants ___insects___
(Par. 3)

Words that mean the same or nearly the same are called **synonyms.**
Circle two synonyms in each row.

. (begin) stop call (start)
. bird (rabbit) skunk (bunny)
. listen catch (see) (look)
. (run) car (hurry) dog

Learning to Study

Number the words to show A-B-C order for each list.

.
_4_ turn
_2_ patch
_1_ bee
_3_ skunk

2.
_1_ carrot
_2_ growl
_3_ happen
_4_ safe

Reading and Thinking

1. Check the answer that tells what the story is mostly about.
   ___ how rabbits hide under berry bushes
   ___ a frightened dog
   _✓_ how skunks keep safe

2. Number the sentences to show what happened first, second, third, and last.
   _3_ The skunks danced.
   _2_ Uncle Bunny heard a growl.
   _4_ The dog ran away.
   _1_ Uncle Bunny met the skunks.

Write the best word to finish each sentence below.

3. We heard the band and wanted to ___dance___. (read, dance, believe)

4. The dog ___growled___ at the loud noise. (growled, worked, laughed)

95

Knowing the Words

Write the words from the story that have these meanings.

1. a place to walk ___path___
(Par. 1)

2. insect bite ___sting___
(Par. 4)

In each row, circle the two words with opposite meanings.

3. (inside) little claws (outside)

4. long (push) hungry (pull)

Working with Words

An *'s* at the end of a word may be used to show that something belongs to someone. Add *'s* to each name. Write each name in the right blank.

Uncle Bunny_'s_   Betsy Bear_'s_

1. ___Betsy Bear's___ burning nose

2. ___Uncle Bunny's___ whiskers

Circle the right word to finish each sentence. Then write the word in the blank.

3. Please ___bring___ your book with you. ((bring) string, spring)

4. The clothes are ___clean___. ((clean) cream, string)

Reading and Thinking

1. Where did Betsy's path go?
   ___to the stream___

2. What did Betsy find inside the tree? ___honey___

3. The bees were angry because ___Betsy took their honey___

Write **T** if the sentence is true.
Write **F** if it is not true.

4. _T_ Bears and bees eat honey.

5. _F_ Bears and bees make honey.

6. _F_ Bees are larger than bears.

7. What do you think Betsy did when she came out of the stream?
   ___(Answers will vary.)___
   ___

97

Knowing the Words

Write the words from the story that have these meanings.

1. grassy field ____meadow____
(Par. 1)

2. very close to ____against____
(Par. 2)

Check the meaning that fits the underlined word in each sentence.

3. The kite sailed above the trees.
____ moved on water
_✓_ flew high

4. Joe is putting a patch on his coat.
____ place where carrots grow
_✓_ small piece of cloth

Working with Words

Write a word from the story that stands for each pair of words.

1. was not ____wasn't____
(Par. 2)

2. could not ____couldn't____
(Par. 5)

Reading and Thinking

1. Check two sentences that tell how Uncle Bunny and the foxes were the same.
_✓_ They were all clever.
____ They were all afraid.
_✓_ They were all good runners.

2. What did Uncle Bunny throw away before he ran? __his cane__

3. Where was Tricky chasing Uncle Bunny? __to Slick's hiding place__
__(Answers may vary.)__

4. When Uncle Bunny saw Tricky behind him, he may have felt
____frightened____.

Write the best word to finish each sentence below.

5. The fox ____jumped____ over the fence. (sang, jumped, sat)

6. The wind blew the ____leaves____ off the trees. (mountain, leaves, sun)

7. The runner was so __fast__ she seemed to fly. (slow, new, fast)

99

Knowing the Words

Write the words from the story that have these meanings.

1. sends out light ____shines____
(Par. 1)

2. between ____through____
(Par. 1)

3. moving up and down ____bouncing____
(Par. 3)

4. small animal that builds webs ____spider____
(Par. 3)

5. homes for spiders ____webs____
(Par. 6)

Circle the three words in each row that belong together.

6. (spider) frog (ant) (bee)
7. airplane (sun) (moon) (star)
8. (tell) (say) carry (talk)
9. small (long) (high) (tall)

Working with Words

Walk and *talk* are **rhyming words.** In rhyming words, only the beginning sound is different. Change the *f* in *fine* to *l, m,* or *n* to make rhyming words. Write each new word.
(Words may be in any order.)

1. ____line____
2. ____mine____
3. ____nine____

Reading and Thinking

Words such as *he, she,* and *it* take the place of other words. Read thes sentences. Then fill in the blanks.

1. Willy sang as he worked. *He* stands for ____Willy____

2. Willy's house moved as it caugh the wind. *It* stands for ____
____Willy's house____

Write the best word to finish each sentence below.

3. I ____ran____ to be school on time. (ran, thought, at

4. The children moved the __toys__ to the backyard. (street, toys, stairs)

5. The ____clock____ showed w were late. (flag, chicken, clock)

6. Check the sentence that tells wh Uncle Bunny would have trouble in Willy Webb's house.
_✓_ Rabbits can't walk on strings.
____ The roof is too low.
____ There is only one bedroom

Knowing the Words

Write the words from the story that have these meanings.

1. lights in the sky ____stars____
(Par. 1)

2. closed and opened quickly ____blinked____
(Par. 1)

Write **S** for each pair of words that have the same or nearly the same meanings (synonyms). Write **O** for each pair with opposite meanings.

3. little _S_ small
4. easy _O_ hard
5. wash _S_ clean

Circle the three words in each row that belong together.

6. (raccoon) carrot (rabbit) fish
7. water (paws) (eyes) (head)
8. (branch) (tree) star (leaves)

Reading and Thinking

1. Number the sentences to show what happened first, second, third, and last.
_3_ Barnie caught a fish.
_2_ Uncle Bunny followed Barnie.
_1_ Two "stars" blinked.
_4_ Uncle Bunny lost his fish.

2. How were Barnie's eyes like stars? __They were shining and__
__over Uncle Bunny's head.__

3. Check the answer that tells how Barnie and Uncle Bunny are different.
____ They both like to eat breakfast.
_✓_ Barnie likes fish, but Uncle Bunny likes carrots.

Write the best word to finish each sentence below.

4. The boat was ____sailing____ on the lake. (wiggling, sailing, swimming)

5. I ____walked____ quietly past the room. (walked, rolled, blinked)

103

Knowing the Words

Check the meaning that fits the underlined word in each sentence.

1. Roll the mud into a ball.
_✓_ make round
____ a kind of bread

2. The bears like to play outside.
____ a show to watch
_✓_ do a game or have fun

Use lines to match the words with opposite meanings.

3. laughing — coming
4. going — behind
5. ahead — crying

(lines crossing to match: laughing—crying, going—coming, ahead—behind)

Working with Words

Write a word from the story that can stand for each pair of words.

1. it is ____it's____
(Par. 2)

2. we are ____we're____
(Par. 6)

3. that is ____that's____
(Par. 6)

Make each word mean more than one by adding **-s.** Write the word.

4. forest ____forests____
5. flower ____flowers____

Reading and Thinking

Write **R** by the real things. Write **M** b the make-believe things.

1. _M_ Bears laugh at rabbits.
2. _M_ Bears talk to rabbits.
3. _R_ Bears scare rabbits.

Write the best word to finish each sentence below.

4. The loud horn will ____scare____ the five boys. (learn, scare, feed)

5. I'll ____wash____ my fac and brush my hair. (light, move, wash)

6. José ____watched____ the man pla the game. (watched, told, knew)

7. We planted ____flowers____ in the garden. (words, ideas, flowers)

10

Knowing the Words

Words that mean the same or nearly the same are called **synonyms**. Use lines to match synonyms.

little — quick
close — tiny
fast — near

Working with Words

A **compound word** is made by putting two words together. Write a compound word for the underlined words below. One is done for you.

A word meaning <u>some</u> kind of thing is *something*

A time <u>after</u> the <u>noon</u> time is ____afternoon____.

A <u>bird</u> whose wings make a <u>humming</u> sound is a
____hummingbird____

Fill in each blank with the right pair of letters to make a word.

ch sh th wh

wh iskers   6. th ink

th is   7. ch ange

wh eel   8. sh ort

Reading and Thinking

1. How is a hummingbird different from most birds? <u>It is smaller and can "park" in the air.</u>

Write **R** by the real things. Write **M** by the make-believe things.

2. M Hummingbirds wear glasses.

3. R Hummingbirds eat insects.

4. R Hummingbirds are different from most birds.

5. M Hummingbirds wear shoes.

6. Check the answer that tells what a hummingbird nest may look like.
   - ✓ very small
   - ____ a box for shoes
   - ____ very large

Knowing the Words

Write the words from the story that have these meanings.

1. scared ____frightened____ (Par. 1)

2. closed ____shut____ (Par. 3)

3. cried out ____exclaimed____ (Par. 7)

Circle the three words in each row that belong together.

4. (wings) head sky (beak)
5. (meadow) (field) lake (land)
6. fit (scared) (frightened) (afraid)

Working with Words

A **compound word** is made by putting two words together. Use these words to make two compound words.

fast light flash break

1. ____flashlight____

2. ____breakfast____

Reading and Thinking

1. Check the answer that tells what the story is mostly about.
   - ✓ how Diver scared Uncle Bunny
   - ____ how hawks fly
   - ____ animals eating lunch

2. Write two things Diver Hawk did to frighten Uncle Bunny. ____He pointed his head down.____

   ____He began to drop.____

3. Write **T** if the sentence is true. Write **F** if it is not true.
   - F The story takes place at night.
   - F Hawks cannot see very well.
   - T Hawks can fly very well.

Write the best word to finish each sentence below.

4. The house was ____quiet____ after the party ended. (quiet, scared, angry)

5. My sister and her ____friends____ took a trip. (field, friends, fence)

Knowing the Words

Write the words from the story that have these meanings.

how big or little something is ____size____ (Par. 1)

one more ____another____ (Par. 3)

very good, fine ____sharp____ (Par. 4)

place where two sides come together ____corner____ (Par. 6)

In each row, circle the two words with opposite meanings.

(down) off around (up)

tell (gone) say (came)

show (large) (small) bless

Working with Words

Circle the right word to finish each sentence. Then write the word in the blank.

My mother opened a ____can____ of soup for lunch. ((can) cane)

Will you ____hide____ the gift for the party? (hid (hide))

Does your new hat ____fit____? ((fit) fight)

Reading and Thinking

1. Check the answer that tells what the story is mostly about.
   - ____ Uncle Bunny's supper
   - ✓ how an owl uses its ears
   - ____ night sounds in the forest

Write **T** if the sentence is true. Write **F** if it is not true.

2. F Uncle Bunny couldn't see Cynthia's ears because she didn't have any.

3. T Owls hear sounds from all around because they turn their heads almost around.

4. Check the sentence that tells how owls and rabbits are like each other.
   - ✓ They both have ears.
   - ____ They both eat carrots.
   - ____ They both can fly.

Write **R** by the real things. Write **M** by the make-believe things.

5. R Owls can hear very well.

6. M Owls can hear clover grow.

7. R Owl ears can't be seen.

8. R Owls hear better than rabbits.

Knowing the Words

Write the words from the story that have these meanings.

1. all of something ____whole____ (Par. 3)

2. having great meaning ____important____ (Par. 8)

3. laughed quietly ____chuckled____ (Par. 9)

In each row, circle the two words with opposite meanings.

4. start (right) (wrong) begin
5. (new) forest trees (old)
6. sound noise (louder) (quieter)
7. (there) (here) now time

Learning to Study

Write each group of words in A-B-C order. Each group of words will make a sentence. Use a period or a question mark to end each sentence.

1. move didn't wagon Barnie the

   ____Barnie didn't move the wagon.____

2. whistles new Children silver like

   ____Children like new silver whistles.____

Reading and Thinking

1. Check the answer that tells what the story is mostly about.
   - ____ Biff's soft red feathers
   - ✓ friends arguing about things that are not really important
   - ____ how Uncle Bunny gets a new red coat

Words such as *he, she,* and *it* take the place of other words. Read these sentences. Then fill in the blanks.

2. Biff smiled as he talked.

   He stands for ____Biff____

3. Mrs. Coats sang as she worked.

   She stands for ____Mrs. Coats____

4. My coat is red, but it is shiny.

   It stands for ____my coat____

Knowing the Words

Check the meaning that fits the underlined word in each sentence.

1. Uncle Bunny likes to take a <u>rest</u> in the afternoon.

    ____ that which is left

    _✓_ time without work

2. The sun went down and I was <u>still</u> asleep.

    ____ quiet

    _✓_ up to this time

Working with Words

A word part that can be said by itself is called a **syllable.** Some words have two consonants between two vowels. These words can be divided between the consonants, as in *pic/nic.* In each word below, draw a line to divide the word into syllables.

1. c o t/t o n
2. a l/w a y s
3. w i n/d o w
4. a l/m o s t
5. m o n/k e y
6. s i l/l y
7. c h i m/n e y
8. e n/g i n e

Reading and Thinking

1. Check the answer that tells what the story is mostly about.

    ____ how Uncle Bunny hurt his ear

    _✓_ how Uncle Bunny slept through supper

    ____ Gordy's loud, clear singing voice

2. Check the two words that tell about Gordy.

    _✓_ friendly   ____ mean

    ____ tired   _✓_ helping

Write the best word to finish each sentence below.

3. The _____fence_____ needs to be painted again. (cotton, fence, word)

4. The new road is _____wide_____ and even. (wide, green, late)

5. The _____nap_____ made us feel much better. (dirt, engine, nap)

115

Knowing the Words

Write the words from the story that have these meanings.

1. touched lightly _____brushed_____
   (Par. 2)

2. makes angry _____bothers_____
   (Par. 3)

Check the meaning that fits the underlined word in each sentence.

3. Something with wings and tiny teeth flew <u>past</u> my face.

    _✓_ by

    ____ some time before

4. Uncle Bunny lost his <u>cane</u>.

    ____ plant for making sugar

    _✓_ stick for walking

Working with Words

Write a word from the story that can stand for each pair of words.

1. I will _____I'll_____
   (Par. 3)

2. you will _____you'll_____
   (Par. 5)

An *'s* shows that a thing belongs to someone. Change these words to show what belongs to someone.

3. bat _____bat's_____ wings

4. Barnie _____Barnie's_____ tail

Reading and Thinkin

1. What animals were in the story

    _____Uncle Bunny, Brown Bat,_____

    _____and an insect_____

2. What did the insect bite?

    _____Uncle Bunny's ears_____

3. Brown Bat didn't want any

    carrots because _____she eats on_____

    _____insects_____

Write **T** if the sentence is true.
Write **F** if it is not true.

4. _T_ Uncle Bunny thinks bats, animals that help.

5. _F_ Brown Bat eats apples.

6. _F_ Uncle Bunny likes all insects.

Knowing the Words

Write the words from the story that have these meanings.

1. an open path under the ground _____tunnel_____
   (Par. 1)

2. something only a few know _____secret_____
   (Par. 1)

3. Check the meaning that fits the underlined word in the sentence.

    I sneezed so <u>hard</u> I fell over.

    ____ not easy to do

    _✓_ not soft

Learning to Study

To put words in A-B-C order you must first look at the first letter of each word. If the first letters are the same, look at the second letters. Number each list to show A-B-C order.

1. _4_ nose   2. _3_ sound

    _1_ eyes   _2_ sneezed

    _3_ mouth   _4_ stream

    _2_ face   _1_ scratch

Reading and Thinking

1. Check the answer that tells what the story is mostly about.

    ____ finding the secret tunnel

    ____ Uncle Bunny's dirty face

    _✓_ Whistler digging a tunnel

2. Number the sentences to show what happened first, second, third, and last.

    _1_ Uncle Bunny heard digging and scratching.

    _3_ Uncle Bunny got his face full of dirt.

    _2_ Uncle Bunny sat down to wait for Whistler.

    _4_ Uncle Bunny fell over onto his back.

Write **T** if the sentence is true.
Write **F** if it is not true.

3. _T_ A woodchuck's home is dark.

4. _T_ A woodchuck needs strong paws.

5. What do you think Uncle Bunny will do the next time he sees Whistler digging a tunnel?

    _____(Answers will vary.)_____

Knowing the Words

Write the words from the story that have these meanings.

1. reached across _____stretched_____
   (Par. 4)

2. small insects _____ants_____
   (Par. 6)

Words that mean the same or nearly the same are called **synonyms.** Circle two synonyms in each row.

3. body (tiny) (small) seed

4. toward (sound) away (noise)

5. (begin) read answers (start)

Working with Words

Write the best word to finish each sentence below.

1. I _____wrote_____ the answer. (wrote, rope, rode)

2. You took the _____wrong_____ street. (rock, rest, wrong)

When **un-** is added to a word, it changes the meaning of the word. The word part **un-** means "not." *Unreal* means "not real." Add **un-** to these words to finish the sentences.

3. She was _un_hurt in the fall.

4. The food was _un_touched.

Reading and Thinkin

1. Check the answer that tells wh the story is mostly about.

    _✓_ Uncle Bunny learning about how ants work

    ____ seeds that walk and talk the same time

    ____ how Cookie Ant became strong

2. How big was the seed that

    Cookie was carrying? _ten tim_

    bigger than Cookie

3. How was Cookie helping the a

    town? _by taking a seed_

    to the town

Write the best word to finish each sentence below.

4. The train went through the

    _____tunnel_____ under river. (mud, tunnel, water)

5. I _____brushed_____ my before I left for school. (brushed, learned, practiced)

6. Take the dishes _____into_____ the kitchen. (under, above, in

119

Knowing the Words

Write the words from the story that have these meanings.

1. sides of the face under the eyes ___cheeks___ (Par. 4)

2. wanting food ___hungry___ (Par. 7)

Circle the three words in each row that belong together.

(nap) (dream) sight (sleep)

fly (chipmunk) (mouse) (squirrel)

(ran) (hurried) (scampered) sat

Working with Words

Write the best word to finish each sentence below.

1. Do you ___know___ the new teacher? (know, nose, noise)

2. Did someone ___knock___ on the door? (nest, lock, knock)

Write these compound words beside their meanings.

underground   sunset   afternoon

1. when sun goes down ___sunset___

2. later than noon ___afternoon___

3. under the ground ___underground___

Reading and Thinking

1. What color were Chomper's stripes? ___black and white___

2. Check two sentences that show Chomper was smaller than Uncle Bunny.

   _✓_ Chomper ran between Uncle Bunny's legs.

   _✓_ The ear of corn was bigger than Chomper.

   ___ Chomper's cheeks got very fat.

3. How are crows like chipmunks? ___They both eat corn.___

Write **R** by the real things. Write **M** by the make-believe things.

4. _M_ Lightning had lunch with Uncle Bunny.

5. _R_ Chipmunks put away food for the winter.

6. _R_ Chipmunks can carry lots of food in their cheeks.

123

Knowing the Words

Write the words from the story that have these meanings.

1. things to learn ___lessons___ (Par. 2)

2. play make-believe ___pretend___ (Par. 4)

3. made a short, quick move or sound ___popped___ (Par. 9)

Circle the three words in each row that belong together.

4. (watch) (look) hide (see)

5. (hawk) deer (bobwhite) (crow)

Working with Words

In each sentence, circle three words with the same vowel sound as the word in dark print.

1. **now** The (cow) (found) the sweet grass and gave a (loud) MOO!

2. **now** (How) can I drive (around) the (mountain)?

Reading and Thinking

1. Check the answer that tells what the story is mostly about.

   ___ a circle of sleeping birds

   _✓_ hiding lessons for the bobwhite babies

   ___ counting bobwhite babies

2. How many babies do Mr. and Mrs. Bobwhite have? ___16___

3. What did the bobwhite babies pretend? ___that a hawk was near___

Write **T** if the sentence is true. Write **F** if it is not true.

4. _F_ Bobwhites sleep in trees.

5. _F_ Uncle Bunny's coat talks.

6. _T_ Bobwhites are afraid of hawks.

7. Check two words that tell about Peter Bobwhite.

   ___ large

   _✓_ fuzzy

   _✓_ clever

125

Knowing the Words

In each row, circle two words that have opposite meanings.

see (close) (far) look

(never) few (always) some

cry break (sleep) (wake)

Working with Words

A word part that can be said by itself is called a **syllable**. Some words have two consonants between two vowels. These words can be divided between the consonants, as in *pic/nic*. In each word below, draw a line to divide the word into syllables.

1. h a p/p y   3. w o n/d e r

2. w h i s/p e r   4. t r a c/t o r

Walk and *talk* are **rhyming words.** In rhyming words, only the beginning sound is different. Write words that rhyme with *spring* by changing *spr* in *spring* to *r* or *w*.

5. ___ring___   6. ___wing___

Then use each new word in the right sentence.

7. The bird hurt its ___wing___.

8. Will the school bell ___ring___?

Reading and Thinking

1. Check the answer that tells what the story is mostly about.

   ___ Uncle Bunny's glasses

   ___ sleeping with noise

   _✓_ finding a friend

Write the best word to finish each sentence below.

2. If you ___break___ the toy, you must fix it. (jump, break, cry)

3. The ___noise___ of the train kept us awake. (noise, rain, floating)

4. Move ___closer___ to the front so you can see better. (later, closer, wider)

Read these sentences. Then fill in the blanks.

5. Bumbles sneezed as he cried.

   He stands for ___Bumbles___.

6. Prickles saw me as she walked by.

   She stands for ___Prickles___.

7. The cane slipped as it hit the ice.

   It stands for ___cane___.

127

Knowing the Words

Words that mean the same or nearly the same are called **synonyms.** Circle two synonyms in each row.

1. dirty (rock) (stone) clean

2. (road) (path) knees   toes

3. straight   curves (looked) (saw)

Working with Words

Words that end in *s, ss, x, sh,* or *ch* add **-es** to show more than one. Rewrite these words to show more than one. One is done for you.

dress ___dresses___

1. box ___boxes___

2. pass ___passes___

3. flash ___flashes___

Circle the right word to finish each sentence. Then write the word in the blank.

4. We ___rode___ bikes through the forest. (rod (rode))

5. The car slipped on the ___ice___. (is (ice))

6. Most mornings I ___hop___ to the carrot patch. ((hop) hope)

Reading and Thinking

1. Number the sentences to show what happened first, second, third, and last.

   _2_ Uncle Bunny and Chubby pushed and pulled a stone.

   _3_ The stone rolled away into the grass.

   _4_ Chubby thanked Uncle Bunny for his help.

   _1_ Uncle Bunny fell down.

2. Because a stone was in the way, the mice couldn't ___make their road straight___.

Write **T** if the sentence is true. Write **F** if it is not true.

3. _T_ Chubby can run faster on straight roads.

4. _F_ The road was already straight.

5. _T_ The stone was heavy.

6. The next time Uncle Bunny hops through the meadow, he may ___(Answers will vary.)___

129

Knowing the Words

Check the meaning that fits the underlined word in each sentence.

1. Did she <u>run</u> in the race?

   ✓ move fast on legs

   ____ what a machine does

2. The tree needs a <u>deep</u> hole.

   ____ having a low voice

   ✓ a long way to the bottom

3. The children <u>watch</u> the puppy.

   ____ small clock

   ✓ look at

Learning to Study

To put words in A-B-C order you must first look at the first letter of each word. If the first letters are the same, look at the second letters. Number each list to show A-B-C order.

1. __4__ stood   **3.** __4__ muskrat

   __3__ sleepy   __3__ minute

   __2__ secret   __1__ acorn

   __1__ safe   __2__ maybe

2. __2__ deep   **4.** __4__ wonder

   __3__ island   __1__ leap

   __1__ bless   __2__ weeds

   __4__ set   __3__ wheel

Reading and Thinking

Use the groups of words in the box to finish the sentences below.

- it looked like a pile of weeds
- he could fix it
- he wanted to see what was there

1. Uncle Bunny jumped on the island because __he wanted to see what was there__.

2. Uncle Bunny thought Musky's house was an island because __it looked like a pile of weeds__.

3. Musky wasn't angry about his roof because __he could fix it__.

131

Knowing the Words

Write the words from the story that have these meanings.

1. a present __gift__
        (Par. 3)

2. with nothing wrong __perfect__
        (Par. 8)

Working with Words

Circle the right word to finish each sentence. Then write the word in the blank.

1. The snow is always __cold__.

   (**cold** fold)

2. He got a new milk __cup__.

   (cut **cup**)

When a word ends in *e*, the *e* may be dropped before adding **-ed** or **-ing**. Add **-ing** to these words. Then use the new words in the sentences below. One is done for you.

   bounce + ing *bouncing*

3. leave + ing __leaving__

4. He is __leaving__ the cane beside the tree.

5. I am __bouncing__ a ball up and down.

Reading and Thinking

1. Check the answer that tells what the story is mostly about.

   ✓ finding the right gift

   ____ standing on hills or rocks

   ____ Uncle Bunny's nap

Write the best word to finish each sentence.

2. The right gift will make someone very __happy__
   (happy, lost, flat)

3. Please __cut__ the grass
   (read, open, cut)

4. Check the group of words that tells about Glenda.

   ____ a very good singer

   ✓ thinking of others

   ____ not a good friend

13

Knowing the Words

Write the words from the story that have these meanings.

1. move the feet in water __paddle__
            (Par. 1)

2. evenly __smoothly__
           (Par. 1)

3. did swim __swam__
           (Par. 2)

In each row, circle the two words with opposite meanings.

4. (close) tiny (far) little

5. soap (last) (first) mud

6. smooth (loudest) (softest) gone

Working with Words

The ending **-er** means "more," so *prouder* means "more proud." The ending **-est** means "most," so *proudest* means "most proud." Add the endings **-er** and **-est** to these base words. One is done for you.

   Joe is the tall *est* of six boys.

1. Donna is old__er__ than Molly.

2. I was the loud__est__ of the four.

Reading and Thinking

1. Write two things ducks must do to swim well.

   __paddle smoothly and__

   __wiggle their tails__

Write **T** if the sentence is true.
Write **F** if it is not true.

2. __T__ Molly was a playful duck.

3. __T__ Uncle Bunny wanted to help.

4. __T__ Donna Duck taught her children not to be silly.

5. __F__ Ducks are always afraid of rabbits.

6. __F__ Baby ducks always know how to swim.

7. Molly was scared because __Uncle Bunny hid and shouted at her__

Write the best word to finish each sentence.

8. Judy __hid__ the keys in the basket.
   (splashed, hid, woke)

9. The girl __waved__ her hand to show she was ready.
   (washed, bit, waved)

135

Knowing the Words

Write the words from the story that have these meanings.

1. surprised __startled__
         (Par. 1)

2. part of a tree __log__
         (Par. 3)

3. part of the mouth __tongue__
         (Par. 4)

Check the meaning that fits the underlined word in each sentence.

4. Does a <u>fly</u> have wings?

   ✓ insect

   ____ move in the air

5. I'm glad the show is <u>over</u>.

   ____ on the other side

   ✓ done, finished

6. My <u>ears</u> hurt from the noise.

   ____ parts of corn plants

   ✓ things used for hearing

Learning to Study

Number the words to show A-B-C order for each list.

1. __3__ shy   **2.** __4__ log

   __1__ here   __2__ lady

   __4__ startled   __1__ glad

   __2__ loud   __3__ like

Reading and Thinking

1. Number the sentences to show what happened first, second, third, and last.

   __3__ Uncle Bunny visited Mr. Bullfrog.

   __2__ Uncle Bunny heard a noise.

   __4__ Mr. Bullfrog told why he sings at night.

   __1__ Uncle Bunny was asleep.

2. Check two answers that tell how Mr. Bullfrog's tongue is like yours.

   ✓ He uses it to eat.

   ____ He catches flies with it.

   ✓ He uses it to talk.

Write **R** by the real things. Write **M** by the make-believe things.

3. __R__ Frogs can make noises.

4. __M__ Rabbits can jump out of their fur.

Write the best word to finish each sentence below.

5. A frog's __tongue__ is very long. (tongue, dress, ca...)

6. Uncle Bunny likes to __sleep__ at night. (sleep, bark, fly)

13

Knowing the Words

Words that mean the same or nearly the same are called **synonyms**. In each row below, circle the two words that are synonyms.

(closer) in out (nearer)

fly (see look) sky

In each row, circle the two words with opposite meanings.

came (slowly quickly) saw

always sometimes (many few)

(yes no) things always

Working with Words

Write the best word to finish each sentence below.

Angel likes to _____ fly _____.
(fly, try, cry)

_____ Spring _____ is the best part of the year. (Spring, Thing, String)

Fill in each blank with the right pair of letters to make a word.

ar or ur

The little bunny grew l__ar__ge.

I ate this m__or__ning.

We t__ur__ned the page to read.

Reading and Thinking

1. Put a check by two words that tell about Angel Butterfly.
   ✓ happy _____ crawling
   _____ angry ✓ flying

2. Look at the picture. Check the two sentences that tell about it.

   ✓ Uncle Bunny is eating the carrot.
   _____ Uncle Bunny ate the carrot.
   ✓ Angel is flying.

Write the best word to finish each sentence.

3. The small plant _____ grew _____ larger. (moved, came, grew)

4. My coat keeps me _____ warm _____.
   (little, warm, friendly)

139

Knowing the Words

Write the words from the story that have these meanings.

1. wall to hold back water _____ dam _____
   (Par. 1)

2. something done wrong _____ mistake _____
   (Par. 7)

Working with Words

Write the best word to finish each sentence below.

1. Storms can bring _____ rain _____.
   (rain, ran, run)

2. Can you _____ say _____ the new word?
   (said, sad, say)

3. I _____ know _____ the answer.
   (now, know, not)

An 's at the end of a word shows that a thing belongs to someone or something. Change these groups of words by using 's.

4. the branch of the tree
   the _____ tree's _____ branch

5. the home of Bonnie
   _____ Bonnie's _____ home

Reading and Thinking

1. What did Bonnie Beaver build in the stream near her home?
   _____ a dam _____

2. Check the answer that tells what the story is mostly about.
   _____ how beavers chew on fence posts
   ✓ beavers cutting down trees
   _____ how to build a dam

3. Check two sentences that tell how Bonnie could use the tree she cut.
   ✓ She could use the branches to fix her house.
   _____ She could use the tree for fence posts.
   ✓ She could use the tree to make the dam stronger.

4. Check two words about Nibbler.
   ✓ sorry _____ angry
   ✓ mixed-up _____ excited

141

Reading and Thinking

Check the answer that tells what the story is mostly about.
_____ how swans swim
✓ how Uncle Bunny goes across the pond
_____ eating carrots for breakfast

Read these sentences. Then fill in the blanks.

Sandy wiggled as she cleaned her feathers.

She stands for _____ Sandy _____.

The clover leaned as it grew.

It stands for _____ the clover _____.

Sal swam as she washed.

She stands for _____ Sal _____.

Working with Words

Write the best word to finish each sentence below.

1. I have a _____ pin _____ on my dress. (pen, pine, pin)

2. Can you _____ ride _____ the horse? (ride, red, roll)

3. That book is _____ mine _____.
   (win, mine, men)

4. Will you feed the _____ cat _____?
   (can, car, cat)

5. The boys _____ cook _____ their lunch. (cook, look, book)

When **re-** is added to a word, it changes the meaning of the word. The word part **re-** means "again." *Refill* means "fill again." Add **re-** to these words to finish the sentences.

6. I will __re__build the house.

7. Who will __re__do these papers?

8. Please __re__fill the tall jar.

9. Did you __re__write the test?

10. Did the station __re__run the show?

11. Please __re__tell the story.

143

Working with Words

Write a compound word for the underlined words in each sentence.

1. A <u>storm</u> that brings <u>snow</u> is a
   _____ snowstorm _____.

2. A game with a <u>ball</u> and <u>basket</u> is
   _____ basketball _____.

Write the best word to finish each sentence below.

3. Be sure to look over _____ each _____ answer. (each ears)

4. Uncle Bunny hid under a _____ bush _____.
   (burn bush)

5. I'll soon be in _____ third _____ grade. (word third)

6. _____ Try _____ to do your best.
   (Try Fry)

Reading and Thinking

1. Number the sentences to show what happened first, second, third, and last.
   __2__ Uncle Bunny's glasses fell.
   __3__ Sunny found the glasses.
   __4__ Sunny pushed the glasses.
   __1__ Uncle Bunny hopped to the pool.

Write the best word to finish each sentence.

2. The child took the _____ little _____ puppy for a walk. (deep, little, clover)

3. Can you see your _____ face _____ in the glass? (family, idea, face)

Look at the picture with the story. Write the best word to finish each sentence about the picture.

4. There is a _____ log _____ in the pool. (school, log, cage)

5. _____ Plants _____ are growing at the bottom of the pool.
   (Flowers, Rabbits, Plants)

6. The water is _____ clean _____.
   (dirty, clean, moving)

145

Knowing the Words

In each row, circle the two words with opposite meanings.

1. (same) cold cool (different)
2. lake (long) (short) pond

Working with Words

Walk and *talk* are **rhyming words.** In rhyming words, only the beginning sound is different. The missing words below rhyme with *shook*. Change *sh* in *shook* to *l, b, c,* and *t.* Then write each new word in the right sentence.

1. look   3. cook
2. book   4. took

5. We took the wrong road.
6. Did you read the book ?
7. I can cook dinner.
8. Did the car look new?

Write the best word to finish each sentence below.

9. I have not seen her before. (send seen)
10. We rode the bus to school. (bone bus)

Reading and Thinking

1. Check the answer that tells what the story is mostly about.
   ___ where Uncle Bunny is having dinner
   ✓ meeting a new bird
   ___ Greta's safe trip

Read these sentences. Then fill in the blanks.

2. The stream sparkled as it splashed.
   It stands for stream .

3. Sal swam as she talked to Uncle Bunny. *She* stands for Sal .

Write the best word to finish each sentence below.

4. The friends write letters at camp. (tell, write, do)
5. Some animals eat berries. (make, buy, eat)
6. Did you drink the milk? (stay, drink, grow)
7. What may Greta do after Uncle Bunny leaves? _____
   (Answers will vary.)

147

Knowing the Words

Circle the three words in each row that belong together.

1. (water) (stream) rock (pond)
2. drive (slip) (slide) (fall)
3. (rocks) (mud) (stones) stuck
4. (he) (she) (it) rabbit

Working with Words

Write the best word to finish each sentence below.

1. The class will care for the bird. (care car)
2. Did someone burn dinner? (barn burn)

Most words add **-s** or **-es** to show more than one. Words that end in *y* are different. In most words that end in *y*, change the *y* to *i*, and add **-es.** Change the words below to mean more than one. One is done for you.

berry *berries*

3. story stories
4. penny pennies
5. puppy puppies
6. library libraries

Reading and Thinking

1. Check the answer that tells wha the story is mostly about.
   ___ how Susie moved a rock from the bank
   ___ Uncle Bunny's wet whiske
   ✓ Susie Otter's new mud sli

2. How long did Susie work to ma her slide? a week

3. Susie said she was sorry to Uncle Bunny because she got him all wet

4. Why doesn't Uncle Bunny like t get wet? He gets cold when he is wet.

5. Check three sentences that tell how Susie Otter is a hard work
   ✓ Susie moved one big roc from the bank.
   ✓ Susie moved plants and branches.
   ___ Susie went down the slid
   ___ Susie shook water all ove
   ✓ Susie moved lots of stone to make her new slide.

1

Knowing the Words

Circle two synonyms in each row.

1. (glad) claw stone (happy)
2. lost knew (rock) (stone)

Working with Words

The spelling of some base words is changed before an ending is added. Words such as *bat* must have the last letter doubled before adding **-ed** or **-ing.** Double the last letter and add the endings to these words to finish the sentences. One is done for you.

cut hit pet
(ed) The dog likes to be *petted*

1. (ing) We are hitting the ball.
2. (ing) He is cutting the cake.

Circle the right word to finish the sentence. Then write the word in the blank.

3. Did you read the sign ? (nine (sign) fine)
4. I heard what he said . ((said) fed, bed)
5. Please get the key to the car . (cap (car) can)

Reading and Thinking

1. Check the answer that tells what the story is mostly about.
   ___ Lefty's missing claw
   ✓ a crayfish's shell
   ___ a rock in the stream

2. What did Lefty's shell look like?
   thin and shaped like Lefty

3. Uncle Bunny knew Lefty was under the rock because his claw was sticking out .

4. Why is Lefty called Lefty?
   He lost his right claw in a fight. (Answers may vary.)

Write **T** if the sentence is true. Write **F** if it is not true.

5. F Crayfish are always friendly with each other.
6. T Shells help keep crayfish safe.
7. What do you think Uncle Bunny might do with Lefty's old suit?
   (Answers will vary.)

Knowing the Words

Write the words from the story that have these meanings.

1. not like most things unusual
   (Par. 1)
2. how long something is length
   (Par. 2)

Working with Words

Circle the right word to finish the sentence. Then write the word in the blank.

1. I finished first grade. ((first) forest)
2. You are too short to reach the top. (sharp (short))

The letter *c* can stand for the sound of *s* as in *city* and *k* as in *cat*. Circle words that have *c* as in *city*. Cross out words that have *c* as in *cat*.

(city) ~~cat~~

3. ~~crawl~~ (cent) ~~corner~~ (fence)
4. ~~across~~ (place) ~~tractor~~ (ice)
5. (once) ~~color~~ (dance) ~~climb~~
6. ~~clown~~ (bounce) ~~popcorn~~ (face)
7. ~~magic~~ (princess) ~~picnic~~ ~~can't~~

Reading and Thinking

1. Number the sentences to show what happened first, second, third, and last.
   4 Tony shot over the bank.
   2 Tony rolled down the hill.
   1 Tony was eating berries.
   3 Uncle Bunny pushed Tony

2. Where did Uncle Bunny find Tony? near the pond

3. Tony was on his back because he had rolled down the hill

4. Tony looked like a rock because his head and legs didn't show

5. Check the answer that shows Uncle Bunny got close to Tony.
   ___ Uncle Bunny wanted a closer look.
   ✓ Uncle Bunny was a whisker's length away.

151

Knowing the Words

Write the words from the story that have these meanings.

. unhappy _____grumpy_____
(Par. 1)

. using together _____sharing_____
(Par. 1)

. flower _____blossom_____
(Par. 2)

Working with Words

A word part that can be said by itself is called a **syllable.** Some words have two consonants between two vowels. These words can be divided between the consonants, as in pic/nic. Write each word below. Then draw a line to divide the word into syllables.

. almost _____al/most_____

. blossom _____blos/som_____

. rubbing _____rub/bing_____

Circle the right word to finish each sentence. Then write the word in the blank.

. Did you hear the _____knock_____ ?
(knew (knock) know)

. I knew that was the _____wrong_____ answer. (write (wrong) wrote)

Reading and Thinking

1. Number the sentences to show what happened first, second, third, and last.

    _1_ Uncle Bunny was eating.

    _4_ Uncle Bunny limped away.

    _3_ Mrs. Buzz poked her stinger down on the cane.

    _2_ Mrs. Buzz flew to Uncle Bunny's nose.

2. How did Uncle Bunny fool Mrs. Buzz? _He made her sting his_ _cane and not his nose._

3. Check two sentences that tell how Uncle Bunny and Mrs. Buzz were the same.

    ____ They both got hurt.

    _✓_ They both wanted clover.

    _✓_ They were both grumpy.

155

Reading and Thinking

1. Check the answer that tells what the story is mostly about.

    ____ Uncle Bunny's wet face

    _✓_ how animals keep safe

    ____ hiding in the weeds

Write the best word to finish each sentence.

2. Please _____think_____ before you answer. (carry, hide, think)

3. We ran _____toward_____ the house in the rain. (toward, over, away)

Look at the picture on this page. Answer these questions about it.

4. Where is Gilda Goldfish hiding?

    _____under the rock_____

5. What is Sunny Sunfish wearing?

    Uncle Bunny's glasses

Working with Words

The ending **-y** added to a word can mean "full of." The word rainy means "full of rain." Write the meanings for these words. One is done for you.

dirty _full of dirt_

1. grassy _____full of grass_____

2. creamy _____full of cream_____

In rhyming words, only the beginning sound is different. In each sentence, write the word from the box that rhymes with the underlined word.

| soap   bright   caught |

3. Late at night, the stars are very

    _____bright_____

4. I hope that I can find the

    _____soap_____

5. My mother bought the fish that I

    _____caught_____

Circle the right word to finish each sentence. Write the word in the blank.

6. We played, _____but_____ we lost. (bit, bat (but))

7. Did you find your _____hat_____ ? (hi (hat) hot)

157

Reading and Thinking

. Check the answer that tells what the story is mostly about.

    ____ stars falling from the sky

    ____ Uncle Bunny's walk

    _✓_ how Sarah Jean learns about fireflies

. Why was Sarah Jean afraid? ____

    She thought stars were falling.

. How is a firefly like a fly? _____

    They both can fly.

Write **R** by the real things. Write **M** by the make-believe things.

. _M_ Stars fall to the ground.

. _M_ Fireflies make lightning.

. _R_ Fireflies are beetles.

Working with Words

Fill in each blank with the right pair of letters to make a word.

    ar   er   or

1. Will you read me a st_or_y?

2. We worked with flash c_ar_ds.

3. She took h_er_ book home.

The letter g can stand for the sound of j as in cage and g as in girl. Circle words that have g as in cage. Cross out words that have g as in girl.

    (cage)   ~~girl~~

4. ~~glass~~ (large) ~~hungry~~ ~~goose~~

5. (orange) ~~gold~~ ~~tag~~ ~~together~~

Write the compound words from the story that have these meanings.

6. thing of any kind _____anything_____
(Par. 1)

7. insect that makes light _____firefly_____
(Par. 2)

In each sentence, circle two words with the same vowel sound as the word in dark print.

8. **soap** Wear your (coat) when you walk down the (road)

9. **grow** I can (throw) the ball (low)

159

Reading and Thinking

1. Uncle Bunny is Carol Anne's

    grandpa or grandfather

2. Who jumped first in the contest?

    _____Uncle Bunny_____

Write **T** if the sentence is true.
Write **F** if it is not true.

3. _F_ Uncle Bunny didn't think he could win the contest.

4. _T_ Uncle Bunny learned something about himself.

5. _T_ Uncle Bunny keeps his word.

6. What do you think Uncle Bunny and Jumper did after lunch?

    (Answers will vary.)

Working with Words

Circle words that have c as in city. Cross out words that have c as in cat.

    (city)   ~~cat~~

1. ~~picture~~ ~~uncle~~ (bounce) (nice)

2. ~~popcorn~~ ~~corner~~ (face) ~~out~~

3. (fence) ~~across~~ ~~candle~~ (dance)

An 's at the end of a word may be used to show that something belongs to someone. Change these groups of words using 's.

4. the clover of the rabbit

    the _____rabbit's_____ clover

5. the legs that belong to Jumper

    _____Jumper's_____ legs

6. the lunch of the grasshopper

    the _____grasshopper's_____ lunch

Circle the right word to finish each sentence. Then write the word in the blank.

7. I can't _____think_____ of it. (think) thank, tent)

8. She _____bit_____ into the apple. (bat (bit) but)

161

Knowing the Words

Words that mean the same or nearly the same are **synonyms.** Circle two synonyms in each sentence below.

1. I (laughed) and Sonny (chuckled).
2. My (path) is my (road) to the field.

Working with Words

Fill in each blank with the right pair of letters to make a word.

sh   ch

1. Foxes **ch** ased Uncle Bunny.
2. Sarah Jean hid under a bu **sh** .

Write these words. Draw a line to show the two syllables in each word.

3. ladder _____ lad/der _____

4. corner _____ cor/ner _____

Add the word part **un-** to these words to finish the sentences below. One is done for you.

friendly   fair   lock   true

The game was _unfair_ .

5. The new girl is _____ unfriendly _____ .

6. Please _____ unlock _____ the door.

7. The last story is _____ untrue _____ .

Reading and Thinking

1. Where did Sonny find Pokey's shell? _at the edge of the path_

2. Number the sentences to show what happened first, second, third, and last.

   _3_ Pokey appeared.

   _4_ Sonny crawled like Pokey, on one foot.

   _1_ Uncle Bunny stumbled.

   _2_ Uncle Bunny tapped on Pokey's shell.

Write **T** if the sentence is true. Write **F** if it is not true.

3. _T_ Sonny was surprised that Pokey had just one foot.

4. _T_ Sonny didn't know that Pokey was in his shell.

5. _F_ Pokey is a speedy animal.

163

Knowing the Words

Write the words from the story that have these meanings.

1. broke _____ cracked _____
   (Par. 3)

2. move up _____ lift _____
   (Par. 6)

Working with Words

Circle the right word. Write it in the blank.

1. Hold on to the _____ string _____ of the kite. ((string) spring)

2. We planted a _____ tree _____ in the yard. ((tree) free)

3. Say the word *bake*. Listen to the vowel sound of the word. In each word below, circle the two letters that stand for that sound.

   afr(ai)d   st(ay)   aw(ay)   p(ai)nt

The letter *g* can stand for the sound of *j* as in *cage* and *g* as in *girl*. Circle words that have *g* as in *girl*. Cross out words that have *g* as in *cage*.

   (girl)   ~~cage~~

4. (gift) ~~village~~ (wagon) (bag)

5. ~~danger~~ (grumpy) ~~large~~ (again)

6. (dog) ~~strange~~ ~~orange~~ (game)

Reading and Thinking

1. Why is the story called "Sam Saves the Day"? _Sam called_ _Uncle Bunny and planned_ _how to save the babies._

Write **T** if the sentence is true. Write **F** if it is not true.

2. _F_ Uncle Bunny climbs trees

3. _T_ Sparrows aren't very stro

4. What do you think Rosie Robin may do after feeding the babie

   (Answers will vary.)

1

Knowing the Words

Write the words from the story that have these meanings.

1. someone good at something _____ expert _____
   (Par. 8)

2. wanting to know _____ curious _____
   (Par. 10)

Working with Words

Use these words to make compound words. Then use the compound words to finish each sentence below.

earth   birth   worm   day

1. Come to my _____ birthday _____ party.

2. A bird found an _____ earthworm _____ .

An *'s* at the end of a word may be used to show that something belongs to someone. Change these groups of words using *'s*.

3. the secret of Sonny

   _____ Sonny's secret _____

4. the nest of the bird

   _____ the bird's nest _____

5. the branch of the tree

   _____ the tree's branch _____

Reading and Thinking

1. Check the answer that tells what the story is mostly about.

   _✓_ keeping a secret

   ___ a worm

   ___ trouble with Sonny's mouth

2. What did Rosie Robin do to find an earthworm for Sonny?

   pulled a worm out of the ground

3. Check the sentence that tells why Sonny was holding his mouth.

   ___ His tooth hurt.

   ___ It was full of carrots.

   _✓_ He was keeping a secret.

4. Why couldn't Sonny share his secret with Uncle Bunny? _The_ _secret is about Uncle Bunny._

5. Check the sentence that tells why the worm can keep the secret.

   ___ Worms live in the ground.

   ___ Worms have no legs.

   _✓_ Worms cannot talk.

6. What do you think Sonny's secret is? _(Answers will vary.)_

Reading and Thinking

1. Number the sentences to show what happened first, second, third, and last.

   _4_ Uncle Bunny's friends cheered, "Happy birthday!"

   _2_ Uncle Bunny saw some strange things happening.

   _3_ Uncle Bunny took a nap.

   _1_ Uncle Bunny decided to eat carrots for breakfast.

2. Write three things that were in Uncle Bunny's birthday cake.

   honey, nuts, carrots

Working with Words

Rewrite these words to mean more than one. Remember to change the to *i* before adding **-es.**

1. country _____ countries _____

2. city _____ cities _____

3. family _____ families _____

4. Say the word *keep*. Listen to th vowel sound in the word. In eac word below, circle the two lette that stand for that sound.

   f(ee)t   (ea)ch   s(ee)d   d(ee)p

The spelling of some base words is changed before an ending is added Words such as *happy* must have th *y* changed to *i* before adding an ending. Endings are word parts like **-er, -est,** and **-ed.** Change the *y* to and add the endings to these word One is done for you.

carry + ed _carried_

5. heavy + est _____ heaviest _____

6. hurry + ed _____ hurried _____

7. merry + er _____ merrier _____

8. hungry + est _____ hungriest _____